"*Cold Fish Soup* understands the oddity, tenderness and brutal ordinariness of small-town life. Adam Farrer is a bold new voice in nonfiction writing. His keen observations are as gentle as they are wry, as attentive to the bleak truths of loss and deprivation as they are to the eccentric humour of humans being entirely themselves … Witty, charming, moving and real." **Jenn Ashworth,** author and Fellow of the Royal Society of Literature

"Vividly documents the minutiae of small-town life on the margins … [and] its strange edge-of-the-world allure … Farrer captures it beautifully." **The Bookseller**, Editor's Choice

"In a book as laced with humanity as it is with the presence of the North Sea, Adam Farrer asks that you fall in love with the overlooked, with that which is crumbling and destined to be lost to the sea. I fell for it hard." **Wyl Menmuir**, Booker-listed author of *The Draw of the Sea*

"A glorious book! Just beautiful. Adam dances down that line between happy and sad with such sure-footed grace. It underlines that there is no such thing as 'an ordinary life', or indeed an 'ordinary place'." **Catherine Simpson**, author of *One Body*

"Such a wide-ranging and thought-provoking essay collection … made me both cry and laugh heartily and fully. It is a love letter to Withernsea and all the people in it that made me love Withernsea too." **Polly Atkin,** poet, academic and author

"A truly wonderful and ingenious writer … funny, warm." **Emma Jane Unsworth**, novelist and short story writer

# Map of the Holderness Coast

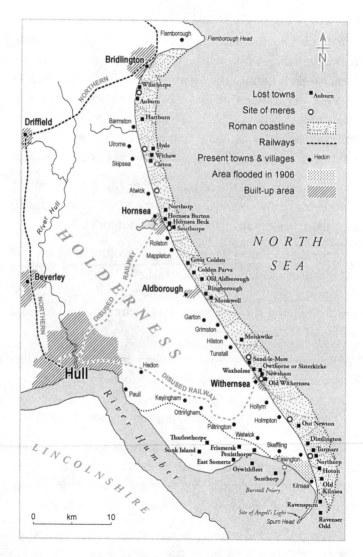

**Legend:**

- Lost towns ■ Auburn
- Site of meres ○
- Roman coastline
- Railways — — —
- Present towns & villages ● Hedon
- Area flooded in 1906
- Built-up area

Flamborough
Flamborough Head

**Bridlington**

NORTHERN

Wilsthorpe
Auburn
Hartburn

**Driffield**

Barmston

Ulrome
Hyde
Withow
Skipsea
Cleton

Atwick

**Hornsea**
Northorp
Hornsea Burton
Hornsea Beck
Southorpe

Rolston
Mappleton

River Hull

H O L D E R N E S S

Great Colden
Colden Parva
Old Aldborough

**Beverley**
Ringborough
Monkwell

**Aldborough**

Garton
Grimston
Hilston
Tunstall

Monkwike

DISUSED RAILWAY

NORTHERN

Sand-le-Mere
Owthorne or Sisterkirke
Waxholme
Newsham
Old Withernsea

Hedon

**Withernsea**

**Hull**

Paul
Keyingham
Hollym

DISUSED RAILWAY

Ottringham

River Humber

Patrington
Holmpton
Out Newton

Welwick
Tharlesthorpe
Skeffling
Dimlington
Sunk Island
Frismersk
Penisthorpe
Turmarr
East Somerte
Easington
Northorp
Orwithfleet
Hoton

Sunthorp
Kilnsea
Old
Kilnsea
Burstall Priory

L I N C O L N S H I R E

Ravenspurn

Site of Angell's Light
Spurn Head
Ravenser
Odd

*N O R T H*

*S E A*

0    km    10

# COLD
# FISH
# SOUP

## ADAM FARRER

*Saraband*

Published by Saraband
3 Clairmont Gardens
Glasgow, G3 7LW
Scotland, UK

www.saraband.net

ISBN: 9781913393465

1  2  3  4  5  6  7  8  9  10

Map on page ii: City Cartographic

*The author would like to acknowledge the financial support
of the NorthBound Award from New Writing North and
Saraband, funded by the University of York.*

For Robert

# Contents

# Jump!

My phone rang, cutting out the music on my headphones. It was my mother.

'Are you okay?' she asked. 'You've been gone for hours.'

She sounded concerned, as if she was preparing to grab her coat and perform an intervention. This would have been an overreaction had it not been Christmas. If someone disappears at Christmas time it's never for a good reason. At best, they've left the house in a panic to source a last minute, terrible gift. At worst, or close to it, they are standing on the edge of a cliff and contemplating their next move, like I was.

The coastline in my hometown of Withernsea is fragile and perilous, built of soft, vulnerable clay. Each day the waves collide with the cliff face and drag a little more of it into the sea. Several feet of these cliffs are lost in this way each year, making them the perfect suicide spot for the idle. I knew that if I stood there for long enough, I wouldn't have even needed to summon the energy to throw myself off them. Just give it enough time and the ground would have made the decision for me, disappearing beneath my feet like a supervillain's trapdoor.

'I'm fine,' I told her. 'I'm heading back now. Millie just wanted a long walk.'

Millie is my aged dog, who strained at her lead while I spoke, desperate to peer over the edge and sniff at the unknown below. When I'd adopted her a few months earlier, it had been predicted that she wouldn't make it to Christmas. Yet here she still was, wobbling onward. The image of me with Millie seemed to calm my mother down. Because really, who kills themselves with their dog? Especially a tragic one. But I found myself picturing it all the same. Toying with the image of me hopping off the cliff, my body descending, my hand raised above my head as I gripped Millie's lead. A Victorian aeronaut attempting to take flight by holding on to a dog-shaped balloon. I shuddered. From the thought, the cold weather and the tiny compulsion in me that was telling me to do it. *Jump!*

'Are you still there?' my mother asked. I realised then that I'd stopped talking and all she'd have been able to hear was the fierce coastal wind and the absence of her son.

'Sorry, yes,' I said. 'I'm here. Sorry. I'll be back soon.'

'Okay,' she said. 'See you in a bit. Love you.'

'Love you.'

This was big-guns talk. We're a loving family but we don't show it in obvious ways. We don't dole out 'love you' unless we're really worried about each other. You get a 'love you' on your deathbed and a few more during bereavements and heartache then, like fine china, they're packed away and kept for best. In this instance my mother's 'love you' meant 'Don't you fucking dare.'

And I wouldn't. Not anymore, at least. I'd been here several times over the years, in this place, or places like it. Places, edges, that had long ago fallen into the sea. I could have easily fallen in along with them but decided against it, and now, it seems, I didn't have a choice anymore. I considered my teenage daughter Effie, safe at home in Manchester with my ex-wife, preparing for Christmas morning and rightly oblivious to the thoughts in my head. Of my precarious position on the cracked rim of the world. She was enough reason for me to stick around. But there was something else too, an obligation I couldn't quite grasp, pulling me inland. The unfinished business of living, I guessed.

# Jump!

So, while I couldn't give in to the urge to jump, it didn't mean I couldn't think about it, and although it was freezing and getting darker, I waited on the cliffs a little longer. Mulling things over, listening to the insistent throb of that tiny compulsion, while Millie circled me, wrapping her lead around my legs. Whether by instinct or accident, holding me fast.

*

When I'd arrived at my parents' house on Christmas Eve, my mother was concerned, worrying about my inability to smile or eat because as a child these were two of the things I'd always done best. 'You used to wake up each morning with a smile on your face,' she'd say, happy that she'd given birth to a being of such relentless sunshine. And because she has always shown love through feeding, it was pleasing to her that I was also a boy who ate everything on his plate then immediately pined for seconds. There was clearly never a time back then when she thought she'd have to consider me glumly wasting away.

'I don't want to talk about it,' I'd said, pre-empting her questions as I made my way into her house, sad and gaunt and making a circus of carrying large gift bags through the door. Lumpy paper ones filled with awkwardly shaped presents and clinking wine bottles. I huffed and I puffed and I fussed and I kissed her on the cheek. Her dogs rushed towards me excitedly and I crouched to welcome them, embracing the giddy, fluffy distraction of their enthusiasm.

It helps that my mother knows that I can sometimes be dramatic. That ever since my teens I've tended to feel things intensely, my default setting during times of trouble being to announce ruin and proclaim that the sky is falling on my head in particular. My elder sister, Becky, can be the same way, making it a well-worn family trait and therefore nothing for our mother to worry about. So, she could comfort herself with the idea that this was just one of my displays of high emotion, and that I'd clearly decided to exhibit that emotion in the manner of a drama student fumbling their way through a scene that required interaction with multiple props. I was all about the bags and where to put them. Chattering about whose was whose. About lost gift tags and the trials of Christmas shopping. Familiar with this sort of behaviour, it could appear to my mother that this was all sound and fury signifying, if not nothing exactly, then at least very little. She didn't know that the death compulsion I was feeling that night was strong and real, and I was having to navigate it just as I have ever since I first began to feel it as a teenager, crushed under the vice-like pressures of my own dedicated portion of collapsing sky.

'Everyone has a worst Christmas of their life,' my mother said, unable to stop herself from acknowledging my sorry state. 'Yours is just happening right now.'

There is a wisdom in statements like this, the ones that remind you to get some perspective during challenging times. But I need them six months down the line. Not in the moment, when it's all happening. When all I could think about was how comforting it would have been to curl up on the floor, dissolve into the carpet and wait for someone to hoover me up. What I want at times when my life goes off the rails is to be told that there has been a big mistake, a clerical error. That I can go back in time, forget that any of the bad stuff happened and carry on as happily as I did before. I want comforting, deluding, distracting nonsense, not words that make sense. So, at times like this I often feel like it'd be a greater kindness to put me out of

4

my misery. Bludgeon me with a spade maybe or poison my drink. Push me into speeding traffic, so I might get to enjoy the comforting escape of a coma. But don't tell me it'll be okay. I know it will be. It always is. It has to be.

'It'll be okay,' she said. 'You'll get through it.'

The details of why I was feeling so low are not really interesting enough to get into. Rooted in a basic relationship failure that I was in the process of blowing out of all proportion. Boy meets girl and they fall in love. Girl breaks up with boy a few days before Christmas. Because boy doesn't do feelings in half measures he reacts as if no one has ever experienced such pain, stops eating or sleeping and becomes a useless puddle of grief and troubling thoughts. Boy's mother tells him to come home for Christmas because boy has called her from the produce aisle of a Sainsbury's, where 'Lonely This Christmas' is playing over the store PA system and he wants to know exactly what kind of psychopath would write a song like that, let alone play it in a supermarket. Boy accepts that his mother does not know the answer, but agrees to come home, disconnects the call and weeps. Old woman in supermarket gets annoyed at boy because he is having a breakdown in front of the milk and she's trying to reach for a four-pint bottle of semi-skimmed. Boy realises this, picks up four-pint bottle of semi-skimmed and tries to hand it to old woman. Old woman refuses bottle because it now has tears and snot on it, tuts at boy, reaches past him and grabs a bottle of her own before bustling away. Boy stands alone in the produce aisle, holding a freezing cold, four-pint bottle of snot-coated semi-skimmed milk and listens as 'Last Christmas' begins to play over the PA, thinking 'This kind of behaviour is why she broke up with me.' It was, as people like to say, a story as old as time.

'When did you last eat?' my mother asked.

'I've eaten.'

'But when?'

'Yesterday?' I said, regretting my honesty immediately. 'Sorry, I meant this morning. Before I set off.'

My mother is brave and strong and stoic and while I am not particularly, I still feel that I need to protect her from bad things. To shield her from any information that I think might upset her, in part because I am her eldest son but also because I wasn't always her eldest son. Before me there was Robert, who was brave and strong and stoic until he wasn't anymore. Until he decided that life was too much and that comforting words no longer cut it. So, I could not give in to my more flamboyant urges and flounce through the door, shrieking 'Mother, fetch me the strychnine. I am bereft and need to die immediately!' before collapsing onto the sofa like a string-snipped puppet. I had to put on a show of being capable. But I did it weirdly because I was still me and I was losing my mind. Just like every time I have felt this way before, I have needed to come home to my family and fix myself, and to do that I require everyone, myself included, to behave as if nothing has changed and nothing is wrong.

'Okay,' she said. 'We don't have to talk, but you need to eat something. You're wasting away.'

This was neither true nor a valid concern, I've not seen evidence of my ribs since the Thatcher government. But it was important to her that if we were not going to use our mouths to talk about our feelings, then we would use them to eat. This was something a Jewish ex-girlfriend of mine had always endorsed.

'We need to *fress*,' she'd say, when life got hard. 'It's a Yiddish word. It basically means eat your feelings.' And because our relationship had been turbulent, the kosher deli near our home became our sanctuary. Our hallowed ground. Where our problems were stuffed into our stomachs.

My family's blood, like everyone's really, is a real mix. We're Jewish mixed with Irish itinerant, Swedish and Scottish. The Jewish heritage comes from my mother's side of the family and it shows. The trope of an anxious mother healing her loved ones through food is as familiar to our home as the sound of my three siblings and I arguing over access to the only bathroom in the house. While my family never referred to comfort eating as *fressing*, the act has always been in our DNA, and it was in my mother when she made a call and booked the family in for a Christmas dinner at Withernsea Golf Club, just a short walk from my parents' house.

'Lovely!' I said upon hearing this news, baring my teeth in what I hoped looked like a smile and not as if I'd just slowly pressed my heel onto a thumbtack. There's a point I sometimes reach where I go beyond eating my feelings and food loses its appeal entirely. When I get like this you could sit me down in a Michelin Star restaurant and I would react to each dish as I'd been presented with the contents of a sun-baked medical waste bin.

I was just wondering how long I could maintain my forced smile when Becky arrived, and it transformed into a genuine one. Her appearance at the front door incited a flurry of chatter and darting dogs. Then my father descended the stairs, calling out to my mother.

'Janet, where's my checked shirt?'

'You're wearing it.'

'No, the other one.'

'I gave it to the charity shop.'

'When?'

'Oh, I don't know. 2003?'

This back and forth felt like watching a tired but much-loved music hall routine, and it was exactly what I needed. These warming and fortifying diversions from the black cloud I'd dragged into the house. And because my family wasn't acting concerned, I was able to settle in and enjoy them being loving, annoying and normal. Reminding me that whatever else might be going on, however I might be feeling or what I might have lost, I was going to be a part of this team for as long as we all lived. The one thing that could not be allowed to change.

Once clothes had been decided upon, we all bundled ourselves up in coats and woollens and headed out of the house, looking like Christmas card characters as we picked our way to the golf club's tired, prefabricated clubhouse. It was here that the brief, protective spell of normality would be broken, and I would come to sit and stare, bilious, at an extra-large two meat roast. Ordering this had been both a trial and a performance. The young lady serving at the bar had presented us with the meal options, solely roasted meat dinners, available in a range of sizes. My mother ordered herself a small.

'We don't do small. We do medium, large and extra-large,' the young lady said.

I could hear my father speaking loudly as he seated himself at a seasonally laid table in the dining area nearby. 'But that means medium is small,' he said. 'That's stupid.' His creeping deafness meant that he could still hear just enough about a situation to form an opinion of it but couldn't regulate the volume of that opinion when it left his mouth. 'Isn't it though? It's stupid.' It was nice to see him this way, difficult and animated. When I'd last visited, back in September, I'd taken him to hospital so he could see a consultant about a list of ailments so concerning that he had been reduced to a worried, grey shape in a waiting room. Now, here he was, all arms and opinions, a blaring disruption in a Christmas jumper.

Becky quietened him down, but the young lady didn't seem to hear him in any case, too focussed on me and my pending decision. My mother looked at me and I found myself ordering a large.

Hearing this, the bar manager sidled over to intervene, tying on an apron as she moved.

'They can't have large,' she said in a broadcasting stage whisper. 'We've no large plates. Charge them for larges and we'll give them extra-larges.'

'We can't do large,' the young lady said, her fingers hovering over the till. 'So, is that a medium or an extra-large?'

I glanced at my mother again.

'An extra-large please,' I said. A bold demonstration of 'I AM FINE AND YOU DO NOT NEED TO WORRY.'

It's strange, this need I feel during difficult times to act in front of my mother given that, as a child, I was completely resistant to any kind of a performance. Especially as it's what she'd always wanted from me.

My mother is a passionate performer, always looking for an excuse to apply greasepaint and parade about in front of an audience. She's in her seventies now but still performs in a dance troupe, as a member of the local choir and as part of a pirate singing group, in which she travels the country roaring shanties in coastal towns while dressed like a drunken sailor. She wanted us children to share her enthusiasm for the spotlight and it was clear that part of her looked at my siblings and I and saw potential for her own merry little band of von Trapps.

# Cold Fish Soup

Being the eldest, Becky was the first to find herself being crammed into a sweat-inducing polyester outfit and shoved into a chorus line. Whether she was a blackbird baked in a pie or the fart-addled rear end of a pantomime horse, she suffered it with the stoicism of a regularly humiliated prisoner of war. Robert was bolder and more cocksure, willingly taking the lead in *Oliver* at the age of ten, his voice pure and bell-like as he performed a saintly rendition of 'Where Is Love?', giving no indication that, by that age, he'd already started smoking and carrying a flick-knife in his back pocket. But it was Becky's plight that interested me the most, because it came with costumes. I was particularly drawn to the flying monkey outfit that she wore in an amateur production of *The Wizard of Oz*. Unlike in the movie, it was entirely brown and topped off, for reasons known only to our mother, with a glitter-specked afro wig. I loved it so much that I insisted she let me try it on, tights and all, so I could pose for a photo. And the image still exists somewhere, of me standing in our living room, cock-hipped and sassy as a tomcat, so effervescent with showbiz pep you'd think I'd just pirouetted out of a successful audition for *Starlight Express*.

But this kind of display meant nothing. You may have seen me happily strutting around our house dressed like Carmen Miranda but threaten me with a stage and I've seen people box-up feral cats with less fuss. I was deeply afraid of public humiliation and failure, an anxiety fuelled by the acute self-knowledge that I was exactly the kind of kid who might somehow wander out in front of an audience with his dick poking out of his fly. So, the fact that I behaved one way at home and another outside of it, dogged in my resistance to the stage, was perceived by my mother as a considered act of screwing with her.

'Come on,' she would insist through gritted teeth, nudging me towards the stage during rehearsals in the town hall. 'It'll be fun.'

But I knew what fun was and it didn't involve a room full of people booing at my adolescent penis. So, I'd hold my ground until she gave up. What I didn't reckon with was that I was absorbing the need to perform by osmosis. That over the years I would feel drawn to stages. First in bands, strapping on guitars and stepping out in front of audiences to sing amongst waves of protective distortion and clattering noise. Then eventually alone, to read stories and talk. And now, it seems, to stand before my mother and put on a show in a golf club. Because growing up in our house was a lot like being the lone non-smoker in a room; you can abstain all you want but given time you'll still end up smelling like an ashtray. And if you spend enough time around my mother then, one way or another, you'll somehow find yourself in stage tights.

The lady at the bar handed us a number of small, laminated tickets, each labelled with the size of our order and to be handed in at a carvery once the food was ready. I looked down at my ticket. EXTRA-LARGE. Extra-large is not a meal size, it's a t-shirt size. It's the size of underwear I buy. I mentioned this to my mother.

'That reminds me,' she said. 'I've got you a three-pack of pants. Your dad doesn't want them.'

'Well, that's something to look forward to,' I said, as we settled ourselves down at the table. Then I realised that it actually was, my future hopes bound up in the promise of rejected underpants.

I looked around the room at the other diners, who were largely dressed in Christmas jumpers and Santa hats, braying with advent bonhomie. Not, apparently, hoping that they'd be the lucky recipients of a swift heart attack or the sudden, blessed release of an aneurysm. But these things were on my mind. These exit options. But I obeyed the family rules: we do not talk about our feelings, we eat them; and we do not leave each other, we remain until time or sickness decides otherwise. So, I was left to sit in my situation and stew, silently praying for a catastrophic biological intervention and if that failed, at least I had new underwear. This was just how it was now. We all had to stick around and see this thing through. All of the things. Life. Relationships. An extra-large Christmas dinner in a wind-lashed portacabin on the Holderness coast. The nausea of it all.

The bar manager announced that the food was ready, and we each queued up at the carvery to receive a teetering plate of food, then staggered back to our table, a trail of dropped peas in our wake. As I settled into my seat my mother nudged me and nodded to the next table, where a man with a white beard and a Christmas tree-shaped hat was just sitting down with his family.

'That's the No.1 poet in Withernsea,' she whispered.

He spotted my mother and raised a glass in her direction.

'Alright, Jan?' said The No.1 Poet in Withernsea.

Everyone knows my mother. She can't walk the streets without someone hailing her from a shop doorway or stopping her for a chat. A cast of characters with shifty *noms de plume* arrive at her front door each week to offer crates of fish or short-dated biscuits at bargain prices '... because it's you, Jan.' Part of this is because Withernsea is a small town, and our family has lived in it for almost thirty years. But also, because my mother's burlesque troupe, the Ruby Red Performers, reached the semi-finals of *Britain's Got Talent* in 2015 and their routine was one that understandably persists for anyone who witnessed it. In a town where everyone knows everyone else, this is at least one way to stand out.

'You should interview him for your book,' she told me.

'Maybe ...' I said absently, picking up my knife and fork and surveying my food, the daunting meat and vegetable landscape of an extra-large.

I'd been given funding to write a book about Holderness – a collection of essays about what it was like to live on this forgotten stretch of the Yorkshire coast. I'd been traveling the area for months, between Spurn Point and Flamborough, making notes about life on the coastline and interviewing people who live and work there. I wanted the world to know about this place and how it felt to be connected to it, to recognise how strange and damaged it was, but still love it. My mother knew that I'd recently spoken to Dean Wilson, a lovably idiosyncratic writer who light-heartedly markets himself as 'the second-best poet in Withernsea' and she didn't want me to miss out on the poet she considered to be the best. I enjoy this, the enthusiasm she has for what I do. She likes to tell people about my work, to point out that I'm doing something creative.

'Adam's a performer,' she'll tell them with a note of pride that causes a mix of self-consciousness and appreciative warmth to rise in my chest. 'He's a writer. A storyteller.'

But she has always been proud of us kids, all of us, whatever we're doing. I could make it my enthusiasm to kill rabbits with hammers and she'd still find a way to take pride in the form and endurance of my swinging arm.

I looked down at my plate, piled high with golden potatoes and roasted meats. Swimming with grease-veined, fawn-coloured gravy. It looked toxic to me. The thought of putting it inside my body made me queasy. But it was Christmas, and this was Christmas dinner with my family and my mother dearly needed to see me eat something. I knew why. I knew what she was thinking and fearing, and I couldn't tell her that she was correct. That, in that moment, I would have chosen the great beyond over a pig in a blanket. But unless you're raised in a death cult you can't in good conscience really tell your mother that all you want for Christmas is for her to shoot you in the head at the dining table, so instead I stabbed at a roast potato and thrust it into my mouth. An act that resembled hunger but was closer to that of wolfing down a foul-tasting medication. It landed in my stomach like a thudding rock, where it rested and sizzled.

I was aware that my mother was watching me eat. There was a responsibility with each mouthful and my consumption became performative, like I was a daytime TV presenter. One of those people whose job it was to stand in a studio kitchen, place a forkful of freshly prepared frittata in their mouth and react as if they're experiencing the apex of a juddering orgasm. But because eating had always been the kind of labour I could really put my back into, being forced to treat it as a trial that needed to be overcome felt like a compounding of my situation. A trading of a joy for a misery. I looked at the meat, which seemed at that moment to be impossibly and overwhelmingly dead. Not a plate of food, but of corpse slivers. The concept of eating them made me feel morbid and cannibalistic.

'Eat up,' my mother said. I avoided the meat, speared a ball of stuffing with my fork and popped it into my mouth. A small voice in my head said, 'Brains. You're eating brains, Adam.' I was aware that the voice was Kiefer Sutherland's from the movie *The Lost Boys*. That my internal monologue had been corrupted to the point where it was being narrated by a movie vampire. But mostly that this was not a good or sane experience to be having. I followed up the stuffing with a floret of cauliflower.

'There,' my mother said. 'That's better isn't it? To have something good inside you.'

I smiled and nodded through bulging cheeks, building up the courage to swallow. It didn't take much, and this wasn't especially noble behaviour. Your family and friends are the people you should sacrifice everything for, even when that includes sacrificing yourself. And really, there are tougher ways to do it. I wasn't having to head off to war or donate a kidney or anything, I was eating cauliflower, which should only really be a challenge if you're a toddler having a rigid-limbed tantrum in a highchair. I felt my mouthful collapse to mush and swallowed. My mother gave an almost imperceptible nod of satisfaction then turned her attention to her own plate.

Her friend Jim was sitting at the table next to ours and he leaned across to ask me about the book I was working on. He was interested in the angle I was taking and the things I'd be covering. I wanted to say the book had changed. Mutated. That it would now be a book about committing to writing a book about the Yorkshire coast when all you want to do is kill yourself. But this was not a time for theatrical displays of honesty, and I found that it was actually good to have something to talk about, grateful for the excuse to use my mouth in a way that didn't require chewing. So, I talked about my travels and my history and the people I'd met.

'You need to write about the poverty,' Jim said, skating a potato through a slick of gravy then popping it into his mouth. 'And the pirates, obviously.'

Jim is a member of my mother's pirate group. He wants the town to be known for fun things, for the sea shanties, the family festivals and community events, but he's neither blind nor an idiot. He knows that the town is dwindling. Fading. Tumbling into the sea. He knows the problems. So, I tried to lighten the mood.

'I've been speaking to a man about a werewolf at Bempton puffin sanctuary,' I told him, my arms animated and gesturing like one of those inflatable, noodle-limbed men you see outside car dealerships on American TV. My movements almost, but sadly not, upending my plate. 'And there's a guy who has been investigating UFO sightings in Bridlington ...'

This show of excitement was enjoyable, making me giddy about my work, and I found myself believing in that excitement. It became a small rip in my self-imposed blackout curtain, letting a spot of light through, and it felt like it would save me if I just kept picking at it. Then Jim upset the thought by placing a slice of rosy-pink flesh into his mouth.

'The gammon's excellent,' he said.

My stomach lurched instantly, and I felt the rip in the blackout curtain close up. I looked down and nudged at the meat on my plate with a fork.

'I'm full,' I said, meaning that I was about to be sick. 'I'm going to wrap it up for Millie.'

I placed the slivers into a napkin, hiding them from my view, bundling them up like a gift, and waited. For everyone else to finish up, but also for the oppressive, suffocating sensation I was feeling to hurry up and smother me. I didn't know then that it would be another two years before we'd all sit down for dinner like this again, and that COVID-19 was about to cut me off from both my family and the coastline I was supposed to be writing about. So, I didn't savour that time, choosing instead to concentrate on the pressure that seemed to be building in the room. A force so great and focussed on me, I was worried it might dislodge my head from my neck and fire it into the ceiling like a champagne cork. This sensation only eased when everyone began rising in their seats and pulling on their coats, getting ready to traipse back to my parents' house, where I would kneel on the floor and praise the quality of our Christmas dinner while feeding scraps of it to my dog.

'I didn't want her to miss out,' I'd said to no one in particular, then I strapped on her lead and the two of us headed out in the fading light towards the cliffs.

*

Millie sat down on my feet and I looked out at the sea, at the bright moon, a circular rip in the blackout sky. I put my iTunes on shuffle, hoping it would land on a piece of music that was appropriately moving and cinematic while I stood on the pouting lip of the cliff, dramatically feeling. I wanted a song that would make this a moment. Help me decide, even though I felt that the decision had already been made for me. But what I got was Prince's 'Starfish and Coffee', a pop song about breakfast. Still, it created a moment of sorts. It flooded my ears. And better suited to dancing than jumping, it obliterated my urges. The lyrics not potent or significant but vital, distracting nonsense.

You can't kill yourself to 'Starfish and Coffee'. You can't kill yourself with your dog. And you can't kill yourself in Withernsea. *You'll be okay. You always are. You have to be.*

# Cold Fish Soup

While no one speaks of them, articulates them, those are just the family rules now. So, I headed back to my parents' house, Millie by my side, her aching limbs grateful for my movement. No longer interested in what lay at the bottom of the cliffs, she pulled me in the direction of home.

# God Hates Withernsea

'Hello from the clifftop in Scarborough.'

Richard Whitely had just begun a live news broadcast from outside the Holbeck Hall Hotel when the scene behind him dramatically changed. There was a brief, low rumble as a huge section of the building broke away and fell from sight over the cliff edge, a cloud of brick dust billowing in its wake. He turned to point at the scene, momentarily flustered.

'Holbeck Hall, a building here that has stood for 110 years, as you can see losing its battle, its grim battle, to cling on to the crumbling cliff.'

The report cut to an aerial shot of the hotel, the remains of it hugging the cliff edge above a great scoop of missing land. Following a night of torrential rain, a 200-metre-wide landslip had taken place, causing 27,000 square metres of soil to take on the consistency of damp sponge cake and slither down towards the beach. This was in June of '93. Our family had been living in the small town of Withernsea on the same stretch of coast for less than a year and for us, Holbeck Hall was big news. I watched this report with no small amount of concern.

'Fucking hell!' I'd said, then blushed. I was seventeen at the time and in the trial stages of swearing in front of my mother. While I'd successfully road-tested 'bloody' and 'shit', 'fuck' was new ground. But she smirked and let it slide, realising that the report had troubled me. 'That won't happen to us,' she said, having been reassured at the time of purchase that it would be at least another hundred years before the sea became a problem for our home. 'We're nowhere near the cliffs.'

What happened to Holbeck Hall was alarming, but at the same time it was viewed as an outlier. A rare combination of factors, it was said. So, not knowing what the future held for us, my mother was more intrigued by the sight of Whitely presenting the news. Having spent the majority of our lives in Suffolk, we only knew him as the presenter of the daytime quiz show *Countdown*. So, it was a novelty to watch Yorkshire TV and see him in this role, as if he'd won the chance to present the news in a charity auction. And because my mother was not worried, I tried not to be either. Instead, I would go on to use this situation as a handy way of geographically pinpointing Withernsea for people who had never heard of it.

'It's near Bridlington,' I'd say. 'Waxholme? Hornsea?' Mentally tracking the coastline for somewhere they might be familiar with. Summoning names of resort towns that are more likely to be mistaken for Dickens characters than places where you might stop and build a sandcastle. Eventually, getting nowhere, I'd plump for disaster.

'Do you remember that hotel that fell off the cliff?'

'Oh, right!' they'd reply, lighting up with recognition. 'You're from Scarborough.'

The demise of Holbeck Hall was a reference that no one loaded with sympathy or fear because generally, no one thinks about the problems of the north-east coast. This is because no one thinks about the north-east coast at all. Chances are, if the person I was talking to had previously looked at this part of the country on a map, it would have been to see where Hull was, then decide not to go there. Withernsea is another eighteen miles further out from that decision, away from the city and along winding rural roads clotted with unremarkable housing and industrial fruit farms. Driving there from the west, the traffic changes from a dense flow to a sputter, as cars choose other locations, the roads eventually becoming so empty you could fool yourself into thinking that you'd slipped back through a portal into the 1970s. Withernsea is not on the way to anywhere, or a region that anyone just passes through, it's a destination. If someone does accidentally end up there, it's likely because they've washed up on the beach having first tossed themselves off the Humber Bridge. So, a lack of interest in the area is completely understandable. Had my family not moved there, I wouldn't have thought about it either. But once we did, its fate was pretty much all I could think about. Of standing on the edge of it when the whole place gave way. Falling to my certain death. The collapse of Holbeck Hall did not help matters.

\*

I'd moved to Withernsea in the summer of '92, and wasn't due to start college until the autumn, so I had no friends and a lot of time on my hands. To fill my days, I'd swim in the sea then walk the cliffs and beaches, trying to calibrate myself for this next stage in my life. And while I did, it was tough to ignore the regular changes in my surroundings. I might sit on a clifftop tuffet and ponder the bleakness of my existence then, revisiting the same spot a week later, discover that it had shuffled several feet down the face. It seemed clear to me that the cliff edge was heading, apparently determinedly, towards our home. I mentioned this to my family and to my mother's new colleagues at the pottery works in town, but no one seemed to be talking about it.

'Don't be soft,' my mother told me, keen to nip this panic in the bud. 'You think too much, that's your problem.'

This reaction just made me feel like a character in a disaster movie. Someone who was able to see an incoming threat that no one else could see, so was dismissed as unsound. The problem, it turned out, was that I just hadn't been speaking to the right people.

*

Spend any time standing on the seafront at Withernsea, particularly during bad weather, and you'll see dozens of people staring out to sea. Generally, they're elderly, many of them bearing expressions of grim resignation, as if they'd all committed themselves to waiting for a bus they knew would never arrive. Others leaned against the railings, watching the waves crash and spit geysers into the air, occasionally whooping like excited children at a firework display. And some are very still and considered, staring hard at the horizon line, as if willing it to snap and unravel the whole world. But common in each, when I'd position myself alongside any of them, has always been a sense of welcome. Hard features would soften, there would be a loud exhalation, and this, I recognised, was a precursor to a chat.

One of the first people I remember speaking to was an old man who'd sidled up to me on the promenade, his hair sparse and precarious-looking, as if all it would take was one strong gust for the whole lot to be blown off his head like the seeds on a dandelion clock. I guessed he'd been staring into storms his whole life, his face so cragged and deeply pleated you could have used it as a change purse. But when he spoke, I learned that one way you got that kind of face was by concentrating on impending doom.

'There used to be towns and villages all along here,' he told me, scything his arm across the sea view. 'Dozens of 'em. All gone. It'll be us next.'

I'd heard this sort of thing before. Tales of the places that were swallowed up by the sea. You could pick up a map of them in tourist information leaflet racks, labelled *The Lost Villages of Holderness*. Dimlington, Turmarr, Old Kilnsea, Sand-Le-Mere. Records go back to Roman times of the coast's inability to withstand the waves, which chomped through acres of land and anything unlucky enough to be standing on it. Yet it was local habit to talk of these places as if they'd not been destroyed, but merely submerged as a whole, hidden by the rising sea levels. I imagined a future Withernsea in the same way, sitting intact under brown waters. An East Yorkshire Atlantis with a bustling bingo hall, bubbles rising from the barnacled caller's mouth as he yells out 'Two fat ladies'.

'They say that you can see the tip of Owthorne church tower at low tide,' he said. 'And sometimes, during storms, you can hear the bells ringing.' He fell silent, staring out into the spray. I followed his eyeline and squinted, both of us imagining a plaintive, ghostly clang. He pulled his coat tighter around him. 'Course, it's a load of bollocks,' he said, laughing, patting me on the shoulder. 'But you keep looking, lad.'

I knew that it was nonsense, but I liked the idea all the same. Stories like this are a charming testament to the human capacity not only for producing bullshit but for swallowing great steaming handfuls of it and asking for more. To me though, it was the details of grim reality that really captured my imagination. I'd been told that when the graveyards fell, skeletons appeared on the cliff face, poking out like chunks of hazelnut in a chocolate bar. The morbid part of me longed to see something like that when I walked the beach and looked up at the coastline, but all I ever saw was exposed pipework. Collapsed outbuildings. Crumpled static caravans slumped on the cliff edge, like aspirational suicide victims, too depressed and exhausted to even throw themselves over. These are the kinds of sights that you can still see all along the Holderness coast.

It stretches for thirty-eight miles, from the storybook chalk cliffs of Flamborough Head down to the Spurn Point nature reserve, where you can find an abundance of brown-tail moth caterpillars and, sometimes, a bloated dolphin corpse. Spurn Point is a three-mile-long arc of land, reaching out into the mouth of the Humber estuary, partially built from the eroded cliffs that have washed down from the rest of this coastline. Walk along its beaches and you are more than likely treading on the ground-down and transported remains of a once happy and laughter-filled family home that succumbed to the sea generations earlier. The composer Vaughan Williams wrote 'Andante sostenuto (Spurn Point)' after visiting there – a swooning and pastoral piece, it suggests he did not encounter a dead dolphin or stand contemplating the bleak provenance of the sands while a determined storm attempted to blow his head from his shoulders. But for me, admiring the beauty of Spurn Point while knowing how it came to be began to seem perverse, like severing your carotid artery then using your final minutes of life to applaud the elegant way that your blood pools around your body.

'Don't be weird,' my mother would say when I voiced my concerns in this way. 'It's fine, someone will do something.'

'But it is like that!' I'd tell her. 'It's like that woman with the steamroller!'

My mother claims to have known a woman who was run over and killed by a steamroller while riding her moped. She'd been traveling through temporary traffic lights just ahead of it when the sequence malfunctioned and showed green in both directions. She was forced to brake by another vehicle heading towards her and while she panicked and contemplated her next move the steamroller gradually caught up with her.

'There she was,' my mother would say. 'Flat as a pancake, squashed into the tarmac with her bike.'

The improbability of this story is great, and I dare say it was told to me as a moral lesson. My mother has lots of stories like this. The boy whose eyes fell out while headbanging to heavy metal music. The musician who was impaled on his drum stool in a prank gone wrong. Whatever point the steamroller story was intended to make, it was lost on me when I chose to take it literally. And it's the visual that most often comes to me when I consider the predicament facing the people of Withernsea. The threat of erosion is devastating but there is time to avoid it. It's not so fast that nothing can be done about it, but instead, people have just decided to wait and hope that it does not kill them.

In 1997, I decided not to wait. Exhausted by the anxiety that I was one day going to wake up and find myself in the sea, I moved inland to Manchester. In my absence the sea did to the land what it has always done: consumed it. When I moved away, the edge of the cliff was still a few minutes' walk from my parents' house. On each trip back home, I'd be shocked by the change, in the way that you are when you visit a child or an elderly relative after a prolonged absence.

'Fucking hell,' I said on my first visit back, looking towards the cliffs. 'Didn't there used to be a road over there?'

'Never mind that,' my mother said. 'Watch your language.'

With every subsequent visit home the edge was noticeably closer and the assurances about being 100 years away from threat were starting to feel much less bankable. At the time of writing I reckon that, with a fair wind and the right dose of indignant anger, I could kick a football from our front lawn and into the sea. In a few years it's likely that the ball would be able to float away of its own volition, because our garden will be on the beach. It's hard to watch the rate at which this coastline is being dashed into the sea and not imagine a near future where the United Kingdom has been reduced to an aspirin-sized speck on the world map, labelled Birmingham.

'You should sell up,' I'd tell my mother on my regular phone calls back home, urging her and my father to move inland.

'You're like a broken record,' she'd say. 'It'll be fine, they won't just let these houses fall into the sea.'

'They let Holbeck Hall fall into the sea!'

'They didn't *let* it, it just happened. Sometimes bad things just happen.'

But I wouldn't be told. Back in Manchester, I began researching the rates of erosion, sifting through government reports, geographical studies and dusty old self-published books on East Yorkshire history. I learned that several miles of coast had been lost over the centuries and that also, I was not unique in my concern. Look through historical records, pick an era and you'll always find someone like me, freaking out. They could be a concerned Roman administrator or a medieval fisherman mourning a lost tavern. Or the Georgian vicar who stood on the remnants of his clifftop graveyard watching a pair of robins building their nest in a newly exposed human skull and calmly noted in his parish journal that the situation, in words more appropriate to his time and station, was extremely fucked up. Sitting at my kitchen table with my stack of printed-out reports and a laptop bearing a boringly sanitary browser history, I realised I was one of those people and deeply committed to becoming my generation's Withernsea crank.

What I was learning confirmed what everyone already knew about this town, which was that they have always let houses fall into the sea and there's no reason why our era should be any different. Still, there is an almost determined lack of concern amongst the people in Withernsea. A crocodile could be eating them alive from the feet and they'd still be insisting that everything was fine even as their heads disappeared down its throat. They're not fools, they know the truth: they'd just rather not think about it. It's unfair of me to expect people to look around at everything they know and love and admit that none of it is permanent and everything is doomed. It's much easier for them to consider lost undersea villages while they watch in real time as the buildings crumble into the waters. But for me, with the luxury of distance, it's frustrating. Especially as a very tangible indication of what is about to happen to Withernsea is already taking place in the village of Skipsea a couple of miles down the road.

Make your way past the picturesque houses and over to the sands and Skipsea becomes a post-apocalyptic land of ill-fated buildings and roads to nowhere. What remains of the former main road now fringes the cliff edge like a string of tattered bunting. The sea is drilling through the clay, revealing layers of peat and post-glacial forests in the cliff face on its way to consuming the few remaining houses in its path. And its appearance sings of all the things that are to come in Withernsea, exposing the fallacy of any comforting ideas that someone will step in and do something. To the south of Withernsea, beyond the sea wall and rock armour, an embayment has already begun, one that will not stop until it hits cretaceous chalk. To get to that, Withernsea first has to fall.

Working my way through my research materials, I occasionally found myself thinking of the old shelter in Hull station for the 76 bus to Withernsea. For many years it bore a piece of graffiti, scrawled in black marker: 'GOD HATES WITHERNSEA'. Catching this bus home from college, I'd occasionally wonder how it would feel to be one of those religious people who viewed natural disasters as visceral evidence of God's fury at decadent human behaviour. To be the sort of person who'd watch their grandparents' house teetering on the edge of a cliff and think 'Woah, what has Nan been up to?'

After all, it's local legend that God has form in this part of the country. Like with Ravenser Odd, a place I'd come across while reading up on the history of lost towns. It began as a sand bed that rose from the mouth of the Humber during the twelfth century and soon after was established as a renegade port and a vile pirate haven, which spent the best part of a century aggressively leeching business from Grimsby and Hull. Its existence was believed to have so angered God that he destroyed it with a storm known as *Grote Mandrenke*, Low Saxon for 'Great Drowning of Men', remodelling the region entirely and killing 25,000 people in the process.

When my mother committed the 'unholy' act of joining a mature burlesque troupe and began a post-retirement career touring the clubs, I let this concern about a capricious, conservative God get the better of me, and phoned her up.

'You should sell up,' I told her again, this time insistent.

'Don't worry,' she said, airily. 'We'll be dead before the house falls in the sea.'

'Is that supposed to make me feel better?'

'No, we'll be dead. Why would that make you feel better?'

'I feel like we've got a little off topic.'

'Ooh, I've not had a Topic for years. Do you think they still sell them?'

'You're doing this on purpose aren't you?'

'Yes.'

So, I changed tack and brought up Ravenser Odd, at which point she brightened up.

'Oh, I was in a play about that once,' she said, referencing a production from her time in a Withernsea amateur dramatics group. 'I played a Groyne.'

'Of course you did.'

\*

Her responses would become less flippant in the late 2000s, when it became clear that several houses in south Withernsea were in imminent danger, including her own home. A committee was formed, the local MP petitioned, and my parents added their voices to the campaign.

'Something needs to be done!' they yelled at protest meetings, along with their neighbours, all engaged with a pressing issue and no longer believing in fine. It may have taken 2000 years, but it seemed that finally, erosion had become an overnight success. Emboldened by her place at the heart of a movement, my mother collared her MP about the issue at one of his street surgeries, then phoned to tell me all about it, still salty with outrage.

'He said that if you buy a property at the seaside you should expect that it'll fall into the sea at some point. Then he said that there's no money for sea defences and that I just need to "get used to it". Anyway, your sister complained about it on Facebook and tagged him in, so we'll see what happens.'

What happened was that she received a letter from her MP, apologising for his tone, but the line remained the same: there was no money for Withernsea. *Get used to it.* Instead, protesters were fended off with terms like collateral damage and inevitable environmental change. Words that are of no comfort when you're faced with the prospect of paying the mortgage on a home that is lying on the beach, more closely resembling a dropped pie than a four-bed semi with well-appointed gardens.

After their protests refused to die down and the MP's thoughts moved to those of re-election, a new response emerged. 'The council is looking into funding for sea defences,' and word got out that an EU grant had been secured. The pressure group dissipated, and all was calm again. But I had little faith in the notion of this funding; it was a mantra that I'd heard many times throughout the years, as plans were made then unmade. Money has rarely been available for declining towns like Withernsea, so instead the people are offered hope. This has meant, in short, that the people there have fallen into a long-term abusive relationship with the concept of sea defences.

Trawling social media for contemporary accounts of people affected by the lack of a sea wall, I discovered Angela, who lived at the Golden Sands Holiday Park, just across the road from my parents' home. Each day she would tweet images of her chalet and its accompanying view. There are shots of a double rainbow, dramatic sunsets but, most alarmingly, of her chalet resting on the lip of the cliffs, ready to fall at any moment. It was Holbeck Hall minus the press attention. So, I sent her a message asking if she'd mind me paying her a visit. She agreed, and when I pulled into the car park a few days later and almost drove off the edge of the cliff while backing into a space, I knew I had come to the right person.

I tapped on the door of Angela's chalet and introduced myself. 'Hello,' she replied, shaking my hand, and with the same breath announced, 'Next door's just been condemned.'

I looked to my left and saw a cooker and a number of boxes waiting to be placed on a van. It looked fine, just like all of the other remaining chalets. The problem was what was behind it. Or rather what had once been behind it but had just fallen into the sea, making the chalet too precarious to survive and destined for demolition.

Angela invited me into her home, a neatly ordered space the approximate size of a one-car garage, and into the small area that functioned as her living room. We sat on opposite sides of the building but were still close enough that we could have played patty cake, each of us perched on a section of a modular sofa. She began telling me about her life and I learned that before she moved to Golden Sands she'd worked for English Heritage, portraying a sixth-century physician whose job it was to form mocked-up dog turds into amulets that purported to ward off diarrhoea. Now she lives off her savings and spends her days blending hearty soups, wandering the quiet southern end of Withernsea and embracing the risks of her existence.

'Two things you need to know about me are that I hate heights and I can't swim,' she said. 'I had reoccurring nightmares about falling off a cliff. So, this is a way of confronting that. It seems odd but I've never been happier. I like being on the edge. People ask me why I don't move over there,' she said, gesturing to the safer chalets on the other side of the site's access road. 'But it wouldn't be the same if I didn't have all this behind me.' She meant the view, the lack of anything else behind her, rather than the peril. 'Lying in bed, I like to think that no one in the world has their head closer to the sea than I do.'

To most people, this would seem like madness and Angela knew it, but she had an acute awareness of the small details of her environment, the ones that indicated big changes. Each day she walked the coastline, looking out for hairline cracks or subtle tilts in the cliff edge, knowing the signs of a forthcoming collapse. This was her second chalet, the first having been lost to the sea during the previous winter. The park has lost many homes and when she took me on a tour of the site, she pointed out a number of heaped, overgrown rectangular patches of weeds next to the edge, where now-demolished homes once stood.

'I call them "chalet graves",' she said, smiling sheepishly. 'That's a bit dark, I know.'

'No,' I replied. 'It's perfect.'

'I never really got to visit mine. When my first place went, I thought that it'd at least live on as a patch of plants but, well,' she said, pointing at an area several metres out to sea, to an absence, 'it's there now.'

We walked down to the place where the chunk of land had fallen away behind next door's chalet, taking some of the perimeter fence with it. When Angela first moved to Golden Sands, she'd calculated how long she could live there by eking out her savings, based on the published statistics for average coastal erosion. She had been told to expect to lose two metres a year, so did the maths and it all checked out. But there is a chaos at play here and government statistics couldn't necessarily be treated as gospel. The section that disappeared next door had easily been two metres deep and five metres wide.

I took a photograph of this area just as two men appeared at the cliff edge and began heaving the fence back onto land. They looked our way. Not wanting to cause a scene, Angela ducked from sight behind her chalet. One of the men called out to me.

'Are you a journalist?'

'No,' I said brightly, heading over to him. 'I'm a fascinated local.' He relaxed then and we got chatting. I learned that he was the owner of Golden Sands, so I asked him about the future of his site, which now consists of a dozen or so chalets.

'I'm hoping to save it,' he said. 'And they're talking about putting sea defences around the edge here.' He pointed around the base of the cliffs. A muddy soup of sea and clay was sloshing around against it. 'But that could be next autumn, so who knows what'll be left.'

I watched as the men shifted the fence into position along the newly formed cliff edge, then said goodbye to Angela. Later, heading home to type up my notes, she sent me a message telling me that the section the men had just repaired had fallen into the sea too, making the rate of erosion now faster than I can type.

The proposed sea defences won't be an extension of the robust concrete sea wall that currently protects most of Withernsea but will consist of rip rap, a rock wall made from chunks of granite, each the approximate size and shape of an industrial washing machine. This is not a new tactic. Over the years, the occasional ship would arrive from Norway bearing a number of these blocks, which are then arranged as a rough wall in front of the cliffs. And each time the sea has looked at these blocks, laughed and thrown them about like hacky sacks. It's a temporary measure akin to shielding yourself from a shotgun blast by holding up a paper plate. They will never be enough; they are only prolonging the amount of time that catastrophic erosion gets to be both news and history for this place.

I spoke to James, who runs Withernsea lighthouse. He's lived in it for the last decade and was, I'd been told, the man to talk to when it came to Withernsea's fate. We sat at a table in the lighthouse café, a map of East Yorkshire laid out before us.

'How far inland would you need to move to be safe?' I asked him.

'Here!' he said, bringing his hand down on the map, like a karate chop, slicing off not only the Holderness coast and Hull but most of Yorkshire. 'All this is built on boulder clay, left over from the ice age. The rock doesn't start until you get here,' he said, his hand wafting in the general direction of York, sixty miles inland.

Later, I phoned my mother to tell her that all of her notions of environmental certainty were built on a lie.

'That's a shame,' she said, wearily. 'Will I have time to go to the shops?'

'Why aren't you taking this seriously?'

'Because we're getting new sea defences.'

'You're messing with me, aren't you?'

'Yes.'

'... fucking hell.'

\*

Some geologists now say that they expect sudden, violent landslides of the type that destroyed Holbeck Hall to occur along this coast every few years. This confirms what people have known for generations: that these cliffs are a conveyor belt, rolling villages and towns into the sea and ensuring that the inhabitants will always be familiar with the rumble of buildings losing their battle to remain on land. As much as the people here might cling on to the notion that it will never happen to them, that everything they love will be safe somehow, in truth, they're treading the land just as they might tread water. Withernsea is as inevitably doomed as the lost places that went before it. But like those places, the town could birth new legends. New bollocks. And in years to come people might say that, if you listen closely past the roar of the cold waves, you can sometimes hear the ghost of a fretful man pleading with his parents to 'Move inland!' while he struggles to outrun the ground, always slipping away beneath his feet.

# Cold Fish Soup

'The first person to see the sea wins 50p!' I yelled, as we rounded the small town of Hollym and made the approach to Withernsea, the lighthouse shifting into view.

'You don't need to shout,' my daughter Effie said from the passenger seat. 'I'm right here.'

'Sorry,' I said. 'I just wanted you to know that the first one of us to see the sea wins 50p.'

'Why?' she asked. 'What's in it for you? If you see it first, you don't win anything.'

'You're missing the point,' I said, though I don't think she was. I think I was. Because I am her father, I was expecting her to be excited about reaching the coast. To react to the sight of it as I would. I was forgetting that the way I responded to the sea wasn't the way that most people did.

*

The 50p pledge had been something my mother always did whenever our family took a trip to one of the resort towns on the East Anglian coast. Withernsea-sized places like Frinton, Clacton or Walton-on-the-Naze. As we'd near our destination, it became her way of keeping us four kids engaged, when mobile phones hadn't been invented and reading led to motion sickness and carrier bags sloshing with warm vomit. For me though, it was something special. Hearing my mother's words, I felt activated, as if she'd released the safety catch on me. I didn't care about the 50p, it was her next promise I was waiting for.

'The second person to see the sea sits in the sea!'

If I saw it first, I kept that information to myself, leaving the glory to my younger brother Ben, who could always be relied upon to go for the money. What I wanted was second place. When my mother yelled her 50p promise, my whole body clenched. Readied itself.

'I see it!' Ben would shout when he spotted the shimmer of water on the horizon, immediately reaching his arm around our mother's headrest and clapping his hand, ready to receive his coin.

'I see it too!' I'd say, hot on his heels and keen to answer before Becky or Robert could, not realising that they couldn't have cared less. Then, for the time it took us to reach the sea-front I would simmer with anticipation, desperate to get into the water. It's stupid I know; I was always going to be allowed in the sea. We all were, that was the whole point of my parents dragging us out of the house and squeezing us all into the car. But I wanted that confirmation, the certainty that, yes, I was going to be allowed to sit in that sea. And not just that, I wanted a guarantee that I would also be allowed to swim, bob, lay back and float in it. The moment we hit the beach I stripped off, yanked up my trunks, then launched myself across the sands and into the water with the hot-footed urgency of a dehydrated man bounding towards a mirage. When it came time for lunch, I would run back to the spot my parents had chosen to lay on beach towels, grab a sandwich then take it back into the water, where I'd stand and eat it while the sun roasted my sea-salted body until it resembled a rose-pink ham. The next few days were always miserable and sore, soundtracked by my sobs as I lay on the sofa in my underpants, my mother basting my livid skin with aftersun lotion.

'I did warn you,' she'd say, but I would have none of it. Just like I have never been able to learn from hangovers or eating at suspect-looking fast-food vans, I have always committed to the sea with the same level of reckless enthusiasm. And while it came with risks and sunburn, I wanted Effie to commit to it in the same way.

*

'But can you see the sea?' I asked her.

'No,' she said flatly, and in fairness, neither could I. No one could. The geography of Withernsea is such that you only see the sea when you are almost upon it, its appearance somehow always sudden, as if it has crept up on you rather than you on it. When we finally reached the promenade and slowed to find a parking spot, I took an involuntary deep breath, remembering the excitement I'd felt when I first heard the news that we'd be moving to Withernsea. When I went on to learn that our house would be just a short walk from the beach, I reacted as if I'd been plucked from a famine and introduced to the extravagancies of the American fridge. Looking at the sea then, as Effie and I pulled up in the car, it was clear that, while the landscape had changed a lot over the decades, my feelings for it hadn't.

'Hello,' I said.

'Who are you saying hello to?' Effie asked.

'The sea.'

'Right …' she said, rolling her eyes as she stepped out of the car.

I'd made big promises to her during the drive over from Manchester, chiefly that this would be fun. That we'd scavenge the beach for fossils and crabs, build a sand sculpture, then grab fish and chips and eat them in a shelter on the promenade while we watched the tide come in. And as we ate, I planned to tell her about my years there, repeating the overblown local legends of the lost villages lying out at sea. What I'd hoped was that I would be able to share Withernsea with her, show her the beach and all the things about it that were special to me, then get to watch her fall in love with it too.

This was the summer of 2016 and a time of change for both of us. I was newly divorced from her mother and Effie was about to commence her final year at primary school. She was ten at the time, almost eleven. That doubtful age, the tipping point when childish enthusiasm was giving way to cynicism and self-consciousness. Once she started high school, she'd be lost to me, and there was no way I'd have been able to convince her to be seen in public holding my hand, let alone a fishing net and a candy pink bucket and spade.

Being her age had been challenging for me, a time when life suddenly transitioned into something complicated and unfathomable. While I was still happily playing with toys and being excited about morning cartoons, my friends began getting girlfriends and were no longer so inclined to read superhero comics with me or go scrumping in the orchards near my house. I was aware that the world was shifting quickly around me and that I wasn't keeping up with it, which left me feeling unsure of myself, unbalanced. I lost the confidence I'd had as a young boy and in its place a shyness developed, which made me fold up into silence when confronted with casual conversation or the unfamiliar girls who had started to appear on the perimeter of our friendship group. I'd felt abandoned and rudderless, not maturing at the rate that other kids seemed to be. The way I dealt with this discomfort was to begin throwing myself into the river.

# Cold Fish Soup

*

The town of Haverhill where I spent my early years was bisected by Stour Brook, an offshoot of the much larger River Stour, which runs through the centre of East Anglia before reaching the Essex coast and losing its identity to the North Sea. For want of anywhere better for us to congregate, my friends and I did much of our childhood socialising on the banks of the Brook. Up until high school I'd enjoyed being around open water for the simple fun it offered. The splashing, the swimming, the throwing in of large rocks in order to enjoy the deep and satisfying sploosh as they disappeared beneath the surface. But when I stopped being able to relate to my friends, the river would become my coping mechanism.

One summer afternoon during the late 1980s, I was sitting on the bank with my friend Stephen and his new girlfriend Leanne, the three of us lighting matches and absently flicking them into the water, enjoying the sound as they sizzled then watching as they floated away on the lazy current. We'd been doing this for a while when something overcame the two of them. A mutual shift in attention away from our shared activity and towards each other. A private act that excluded me. I'm not sure what initiated it. Maybe it was the heat of the flames or the sensual hiss as they were extinguished by the river, but pretty soon the two of them were red-faced and kissing and I was left feeling itchy and out of place. My reaction to this was sudden and instinctual as I exited stage left, hurtling towards the water as if someone had hoisted me up by the belt and collar then tossed me into it. My body hit the narrow strait with such force that the water briefly parted, splashing up the banks and spattering the two of them. They stopped kissing immediately and, once their shock had died down, they began laughing. Stephen picked up his match-box and the two of them started flicking lit matches down at me while I batted them away and into the river with karate chops and high kicks, water sloshing from my hands and feet.

'Hyah! Hyah!' I yelled from the river, miniature kabooms of sulphur appearing all around me. 'Hyah!'

The awkward situation had been diffused, I was at the heart of the fun again and absolutely no one was horny. It wasn't planned, but I recognised a good idea when I saw one and repeated this move the next time things became difficult for me on the riverbank. Here, it became my reliable go to. It wasn't always kissing that spurred me into action, sometimes it was a conversation I wasn't mature enough to understand or an uncomfortable discussion about puberty and developing bodies. And I didn't always *jump* into the water either. Often, I would simply get up, turn away from the group and wade slowly into it, up to my middle, as if possessed by a force order-ing me to do so. Or else I'd stand bolt upright and keel over like a felled tree, slapping painfully against the surface with a concussive, interrupting boom.

Over time though, my desire to enter the water became an independent compulsion. I didn't always need the stimulus of a bad time, my proximity to it would be enough. Faced with a river, a lake or even a good-sized pond I found that it was all I could do to hold myself back, the impulse to leap in becoming as powerful as hunger. If I was lucky, my common sense would wrestle with the drive to throw myself in and I could get past the danger without getting drenched. But it was an impulse that transformed my early teens into a sequence of watery encounters, featuring gripped railings, riverbank trembles and inevitable walks home in squelching trainers.

# Cold Fish Soup

I would go on to disgrace myself during a three-day school trip to the Lake District, when my class hiked up a crag and we encountered a deep recess in the rocks, filled with glimmering, glass-clear water.

'It's so pure you could drink from that,' our guide told us, as he led my teacher, Mr Guyton, and the rest of the class around the pool of water. Each of them carefully picking their way around the slime-covered edge as they continued their ascent. I held back though. Shooting looks at the water. Admiring the shimmering beauty of its still and unbroken surface. Before I really knew what sexual desire was or why my knees would give way at the sight of a woman in short shorts, I knew what wanting to throw myself into water was. So, I did that. Fully clothed and weighed down with hiking boots, I balled myself up and flew, crying out as I destroyed the perfect surface, the water seeming to fizz as I sank and it rushed past my ears. The brilliant cold shocked my body. When I rose, gasping for air, I saw that my classmates were laughing and that Mr Guyton was panicked and furious, slipping clownishly on the buttery rocks as he frantically scrambled towards me. Revelling in this response, I spent a good five minutes paddling around, slapping the surface in an effort to make it look as if I couldn't get out. Mr Guyton roared at me from the bank and, finally, grabbed one of my hands, heaving me out and onto the rocks.

'It was an accident,' I told him, as I sat emptying water from my boot. 'I fell.'

'People who are falling,' he said, his lips thin and white, 'do not generally yell "*Cannonball!*"'

I would go on to 'fall' from rowing boats, off bridges, over the fence and into a river during a trip to Cockley Cley medieval village. Back in Haverhill I found any excuse to lose balance on the banks of Stour Brook so I could stride through the water and marvel at the sight of my limbs beneath the surface, appearing as if they'd been trapped in wobbling, mulch-coloured jelly. Then I'd slop my way home, reeking of stagnant water, to decant globs of frogspawn into our tropical fish tank, where they would cause contamination and death.

'What is wrong with you?' my father would ask, scooping angelfish corpses from the water with a small hand net. I'd struggle to reply, too busy wondering if I was small and flexible enough to squeeze into the tank.

In what seemed like an effort to channel my water compulsion into something positive and athletic, my parents booked me onto a canoeing course during the summer of '89, where I was taught how to roll my canoe upright should I be unlucky enough to overturn it. I was then let loose at a water park and rowed my way out to the middle of a lake to test out my new skill, capsizing and righting my canoe over and over. Churning up the water like the wheel on a paddle steamer.

'What is *wrong* with you?' my mother asked, learning of my behaviour when she came to pick me up.

'I'm clumsy?' I'd said, deciding that I needed an answer to this question, even if it wasn't a very good one.

'Well, you're definitely something,' she'd said, likely trying to recall if she'd managed to concuss me as a baby during a crucial developmental stage. What she feared, I think, was that she had another problem child on her hands. In the twenty-first century we've found kinder ways to address matters like this. Kinder words, certainly. My elder brother Robert, for example, had been fond of dangling himself from road bridges and pissing onto traffic as it hurtled along beneath him. At the time, this was treated as delinquency, but our family now recognises

44

it as a symptom of his undiagnosed ADHD. For my part, I have been told that my urge to risk drowning at every opportunity was a localised form of obsessive-compulsive disorder, but I never saw it that way. I didn't think something bad would happen if I didn't submerge myself. That my loved ones were at risk or that the sun would explode if I wasn't up to my eyes in a canal. It was more of a desire to return to the water and enjoy something I'd discovered about myself when I was in it. What had started as a way of avoiding awkward situations and getting attention had evolved into something special for me. At first, I had required an audience to feel this sensation but as time went on, I found that I only needed the water.

There were days when I would wander off into the Suffolk countryside alone, following the course of Stour Brook in search of broader, deeper stretches where I could lower myself into the water and listen to the babble and plop as it slipped past me and all the other obstructions it encountered on its journey to the sea. I'd hold my hands out at my sides and try to stand as still as a rock, enjoying the force of the current, the unstoppability of it, as it crashed into my palms and leapt over them in small, glassy waves. I soon developed an awareness that, for me, there was solace and sanctuary in the water. It was a space I could escape to, a changed environment with a different set of rules to the land. Up to my neck in water, I felt shielded. Not warm or cold but pleasingly, protectively numb. At that depth there was also an equality; we're all the same if we go deep enough, just bobbing heads, our bodies foreshortened and obfuscated. I found that I liked myself better when I was in wild, open water and this was why, on the day we moved to Withernsea, the beach had been my first port of call.

# Cold Fish Soup

*

While my parents were busy sifting through cardboard boxes and unpacking essentials, I slipped away to the cliffs with our dog, Daisy, a gangly Labrador/whippet cross. We headed down the weathered concrete steps that led to the sands, my steps hurried, keen to acquaint myself with the place where I planned to spend most of my time. I let Daisy off her lead and watched as she gambolled away across the wet sands, her long legs making her look coltish and uncoordinated at first. But when she reached the sea, she looked as if she belonged in it, becoming giddy and joyous. She hurled herself around in the shallows, biting at the waves and spume, running in wild circles as arcs of water whipped from her tail. I wondered if this was how I looked to other people when I encountered water. Not graceful or amusing, but wild and demented. It didn't bother me in any case, my overriding feeling as I watched her being one of envy.

Before we'd made the move to Withernsea, our whole family had taken a trip there to get the measure of the place and we stopped for a snack in a seafront café, where my mother soon got chatting to a talkative, elderly woman. She'd been sitting at the table next to ours and became too intrigued by our jarringly out-of-town voices to let us enter her orbit without investigation. After some small talk about where we were from and why we were in town, the two of them got on to the topic of the sea.

'People are funny about swimming here,' the old woman had said, explaining that not many people looked at the coast of Withernsea with a sense of longing. The water closest to the coastline is coloured by the eroding clay cliffs, giving it the murky quality of under-milked tea. 'They worry about sewage,' she said, adding that some holidaymakers tended to look at the sea and picture the source of its colour to be a huge undersea soil pipe, belching a continuous stream of hideous turds into the waters. So, they shied away from venturing into it, out of the fear that they'd emerge as filthy as a seabird caught up in an oil disaster.

'It isn't dirty though,' the woman assured us. 'It's just full of clay.'

I thought this sounded like a pretty neat definition of dirty water, but for someone wired like me it was never going to be a problem. The fact that no one else was in it was part of its charm. What could be more of a luxury than your own private sea? This was how I'd seen it on that first day, this expanse of water, no one in it but my dog. And shortly thereafter, my dog and me. I took off my trainers and socks then ran into the water. Clothed in jeans and a t-shirt but still shocked by the jolting cold of the North Sea, which even in July tends to greet bathers with more of a slap than a kiss.

My mother had always taught me to acclimatise to the sea in stages. First to put my feet in, then my hands, before wading in at intervals. Knees, hips, chest, shoulders, pausing at each step to centre my breathing and swat at my body with handfuls of water, dowsing myself. Adjusting. I dunked my hands, filtering the water through my fingers and watching it fall like bands of fogged, amber glass. When I looked down though, I couldn't see through it at all, my legs appearing as if they'd been severed at the knee and that I was miraculously walking the rust-coloured surface on stumps. Everything below that point was a mystery. I could have been entirely safe or millimetres away from being savaged by flesh-snipping crabs. But I felt no threat or concern. Being in the North Sea had given way to something I'd felt in rivers before, but never so strongly: an even deeper sense of cradling comfort. I absorbed the smell and the grit, the way it made my body bristle with activity, the saltwater shimmying into my pores, thrilled at the knowledge that I'd later get to enjoy the sensation of it crisping and tightening on my skin as it dried. Even though, to the sea, I was insignificant, I felt like I fully existed when I was in it. Alive in a way I never felt on land. I wanted more of that and before long I was up to my chest, my pockets filling with sand and seaweed. I knew that I was in too deep but also that, for me, there had become no such thing.

When Daisy and I arrived home a couple of hours later, soaked and guilty, my mother just looked at us and sighed, no longer bothering to ask what was wrong with me. Knowing that what I'd done had been inevitable.

'Dry the dog off and get changed,' she'd said, turning to fill a drawer with cutlery. 'There's a box of clothes in your room.'

For the rest of that summer, I repeated this pattern, exploring the coastline and testing my mother's patience. Never fully dry, always leaving a trail of sand and damp footprints behind me. So, it was a relief to her when September rolled around, and it became time for me to attend college in Hull.

I hadn't been quick to make new friends. In fact, I made none. I'd turned up with new clothes and a curious accent, hoping this would do the work for me and draw people in, too shy and self-conscious to reach out to others and risk rejection. When this didn't work, I chose to reject other people, convincing myself that loneliness was a considered choice I'd made. I kept my head down in classes and left the campus at break times to walk the banks of the Holderness Drain, a grim manmade river that ran past my college, and toy with the idea of throwing myself into it. I knew that this was not a sustainable plan, so each morning, as I headed along Withernsea promenade to catch my bus to Hull, I would think of ways to improve my situation. If I could find a means to become more confident and forthright, to reinvent myself, then people might be drawn to me. But more often than not, I would become distracted from these thoughts by the sea. Scanning the surface for the sight of an old man who I'd see swimming in it each morning.

Regardless of the weather he'd be out there, his bald, white head bobbing along like a lost football. Occasionally he would disappear under the curl of a wave and I'd hold my breath, wondering if I might become the sole witness to his death. But then he'd emerge, his mouth yawning for air, arms powering forward. *He's got it made*, I thought, enviously. *He knows exactly who he is.* Over the weeks I learned that I could use this man like a timepiece, so reliable was his progress through the waters. If he was level with the fishing lake, I was making good time. If he was nearing the lifeboat station, I was in danger of missing my bus and needed to pick up my pace. Then, sometime during that first winter in Withernsea, I looked out for him and found that he wasn't there. I didn't think too much of it at first, but after I didn't see him for a few more days I mentioned him to my mother.

'Oh, he died,' she said, having heard about his fate from one of her colleagues at the pottery works. 'It was quite sad. They found him on the beach, just lying there in his trunks.'

I should have recognised the sadness in this, but I was too distracted by what I saw as a job opportunity opening up. I didn't think about how this man's life might have ended. His legs perhaps snagged in a fishing net, dragging him to his doom. Or that he might have ended his days by being struck in the temple by a trawler. When I considered his absence all I saw was a sign that read 'Situation Vacant' and a way in which my compulsion towards the water could finally have an upside.

I pledged that, just like the old man, I would swim in the sea every day and in doing so I would become a person that people noticed and respected. Mysterious, driven and muscular. Someone else's bobbing football. Their reliable timepiece. I let my imagination run away with itself, thinking of all the awed ways I'd be spoken of by fascinated passers-by.

'I heard he was training to swim the Atlantic.'

'I heard that he swims every day in tribute to his great love, lost at sea.'

'I heard that he was a merman.'

Not wishing to waste any time, I took myself down to the beach early one grey December morning, a towel under my arm, determined to make a good show of this. I chose a spot that was close to our house but far enough away from the bustle of the town centre that I wouldn't have too much scrutiny. I wanted some privacy while my body was still skinny and ill-defined, not planning on becoming a more public figure until the sea had assisted my physique to resemble carved stone.

I stashed my clothes and towel under a rock near the cliff face and waded into the shallows, determined not to ruin the moment by girlishly squealing or shivering too visibly. Not to break my stride by following my mother's acclimatisation regime as I moved into the freezing brown waters, just wanting to appear natural and *of the sea*. After all, private as this was, anyone could have been watching. A poet looking for inspiration. Or maybe a beautiful woman who understood the powerful intensity of brooding male souls. So, I advanced through the waves and as I got deeper and the water closed in on me, my mission abruptly became about something else. It was tougher than I had expected, the sea so much colder, and I had to fight to move, my limbs seizing up from a sharp, gripping pain. *Bear traps*, I thought. *It's like swimming through bear traps.* The frustration of this tapped into a store of suppressed anger and my progress through the water stopped being an exhibition or a route to a new self and turned into a battle. I didn't care about an audience, focusing instead on the negativity that rose as I pushed my feet off the sands and launched forward, driving my arms down and pushing against the tide. I found myself thinking of my stockpile of personal embarrassments and my inability to cope with the basics of life back on land. Of all those ways I'd responded to uncomfortable situations over the years, my goonish behaviour and the awkward silences that often followed it, how unpalatable my obvious yearning for friendship must be to the people at college. I processed an accumulated litany of small, crushing moments that, once I allowed them all to descend into my serious sixteen-year-old head, threatened to capsize me, and, if they did, I wasn't sure I could right myself. What's more, I wasn't sure that I'd want to. It was a while before I noticed that I was swearing as I moved. Not pacing myself. Not knowing how. Just getting angrier as I kicked and crawled. Angry at myself.

'Fucking shit fuck …' I spat, the cold shocking my lungs into breathlessness, making me lightheaded as I sprayed salt and sand through my teeth, swallowing mouthfuls of freezing sea water as I moved. Swearing and gasping. 'Ffucking ffffuck …'

From the beach I must have looked like a toddler having a tantrum in a bathtub, but I didn't care. It felt too important to stop. My shoulders threatened to dislocate. There was a new and piercing sharpness in my chest, but I kept on going, daring my body to give up completely so that I wouldn't have to go back to the land. I pushed harder, allowing myself to pause and sink every now and then. To drown just a little before resurfacing and pressing on once more, enjoying the feeling of being somehow powerful but also small and vulnerable. There was a strange relief in the knowledge that I give could give up at any moment and the sea would just accept me. Tidy me away. I would wonder later if this was what had happened to that old man. If he had started out the way I had then realised he'd reached his time and decided to give in, letting the sea pull him down. I hadn't reached that point yet, but until I did, I fought. Tantrumed.

'Fucking shit fffuck ...'

When I finally burned out, I didn't let myself go under. Instead, I rolled onto my back to lie on the surface. Drifting, panting, sucking for air. Icy water flooded into my ears with a slurp that made me shudder. My head froze. I imagined my body turning from blue-grey to alabaster white, pictured myself laid out in a fishmongers' window, but when I held up my hand to look at my skin it was red and flushed, the blood having raced to the surface. If anything, I looked heated. Boiled. Steamed. But I was numb and painless, robbed of feelings in both my body and my head. I stared up at the petrol-blue sky and the seabirds darting across it; determinedly not looking back at the land, where my problems still existed. After a while my breathing steadied itself and I stopped shuddering, allowing my body to bob about on the rolling waves, wondering if this would be the moment I'd decide to stay in the water forever. No, *this* moment. Maybe *this* one. But when practical thoughts kicked in and I began to fret about the potential long-term effects the water temperature might have on my genitals, it was clear that

I was thinking of a life beyond that day. So, I started the slow process of paddling to shore and heaving myself back onto the beach. Not transformed but different. Not cured but better.

I sat on the sand for a while afterwards, composing myself and rubbing my limbs with a towel to encourage blood circulation. Unable to stand. But I knew that I wanted more and, aching and exhausted from the strain on my weak, overused muscles, I went back to the sea the following day. And the next. Never thinking of it as exercise or therapy, more of a way to exorcise my compulsion. But it had become something else too, a daily act of survival. Every time I stepped into the sea after that first determined swim and made it back out again it felt like a victory over death. Nothing about what I was doing was a matter of audience approval or opinion anymore; I either survived or I didn't.

I kept this up for months, defying weather and tidal temperament each day, discovering that, while I didn't have the kind of body that would get ripped simply from bobbing about in the water like a bath toy, it did improve the way I felt about my life on land. I would eventually sign-up to a different college and click with a group of friends, develop a greater interest in music and girls and visit the beach less and less, not needing it so much. And over time my relationship with the water began to shift. The occasions when I did enter it were often marred by incidents that seemed designed to push me away.

Swimming one late summer afternoon, I was caught unawares by a sudden wave that knocked my glasses from my head and into the sea, where they immediately sunk. Without them, I am practically blind. Take them off and anything further than the end of my nose is transformed into a dappled and confusing blur, leaving me helpless and vulnerable.

I panicked, wildly raking my hands through the waters and clawing at the sucking sands beneath them, hoping to snag my glasses before they were pulled down and disappeared forever. My fingers met with nothing but seaweed and unseen slime, and after about ten minutes of desperate searching, I decided to give up and make my way home. I was just scanning the beach, trying to work out where I'd left my clothes when a man called out to me.

'Need help?' he said, and I squinted in the direction of his voice to see him heading towards me, pushing along what appeared to be a large, industrial lawnmower. It turned out to be some sort of motorised seafood harvesting machine, which vacuumed the shallows for shellfish. The man had been watching my desperate searching for some time and it had eventually become too unbearable for him to not intervene. I explained what had happened and he offered to comb the beach with his contraption, hopeful that my glasses might be scooped up in his net. I stood back, squinting through the shrinking light at his fuzzy outline as it passed back and forth between the groynes, my hope dying with each fruitless sweep. When it got too dark to carry on, he helped me find my clothes. I thanked him then began getting dressed, glowering at the blur of the sea as I tied my laces.

'Fuck you,' I said.

'Shush,' said the sea, as it dragged itself across the sepia sands. 'Shush.'

The next time I entered the water, I left my new glasses on land and, perhaps because I didn't see it coming, was struck between the shoulder blades by a large piece of driftwood. It landed like a shocking punch and I staggered back onto the beach to catch my breath, a baseball-sized welt growing in the middle of my back and a new and lingering sense of resentment rising whenever I looked at the sea. The blow had felt direct and determined, a punishment for my absence and neglect. Of course, I knew it was nothing of the sort. The sea is not capable of feeling hurt or giving a fuck; it is in a permanent state of not being able to give any fucks at all. I had entered it expecting pleasure and an identity, but I'd done so at my peril and had suffered for it. To the sea, beating me with a piece of wood was nothing personal but for me it seemed like that and, consciously or not, it drove me away. My great love had become aloof and colder than ever. So, we broke up and I decided to see other waters.

Without the sea to turn to, Withernsea had little to offer me. Every opportunity there that didn't involve being in the water was slowly being consumed by it. I saw nothing but a grim future for me, so I left town and spent a couple of years studying sculpture in Barnsley, where I began plunging myself into the River Dearne. During the summer of '97, when the heat became unbearable and the stretch of river I favoured grew too busy with locals driven mad by the rising temperatures, I took my towel and wandered the edgelands, looking for somewhere more private. After traipsing a while, wading through tall grass and avoiding the wild horses roaming the fields that sloped down from a disused coal mine, I found what looked to be a good place at the bend of a river. I didn't bother undressing, I just jumped off the bank, feet first, not knowing or caring how deep it was, still calibrated to the depth of the sea. The water was inky black, it could have been one-foot deep or one thousand for all I knew, but I went in regardless, spearing it with my heels. I sank for a long time then clawed my way through the darkness and back up to the air. Small flies flitted about on the surface, bothering me and zipping into my ears and mouth, but it provided the respite I needed from the heat and I eased back, lazily floating. I'd been there for a while, when a group of teenagers appeared at the bank and looked down at me, bobbing about in my t-shirt and jeans. I grew nervous then, convinced that they were about to do something bad from up there. Cause trouble. Maybe start throwing dirt and rocks. But they stayed silent, regarding me with still and curious interest. Finally, one of them called down to me.

'What you doin' in there?'

'Cooling down,' I called back, bracing myself for the first missile to land.

The boy smiled and shook his head, turning to his friends. There was a long pause and I waited for something to happen. For them to suddenly snap and do something terrible to me. Eventually the boy spoke.

'You're mad, you,.' he said, a chuckle in his voice, and he and his friends wandered off, muttering amongst themselves.

I didn't think much of this, and just carried on happily floating, grateful that I'd avoided getting my skull dented by a half-brick then drowning alone in dark water. It didn't cross my mind again until a few years later, when I was sitting in a pub and fell into a chat with a man who'd grown up in Barnsley. After a while, our conversation worked its way to my swimming spot, and he smiled in the way people do when they're about to reveal a delicious secret.

'You were swimming in a flooded coal mine,' he told me. 'They're so deep, you can hide anything in them.'

By anything it transpired that he meant dead bodies, the popular rumour being that this area was full of them. Enemies and love rivals, murdered, weighted down with chains or sacks of rocks then tossed into the black river, sinking deeper than any man could dive. What these lads had seen when they looked down at me from the bank was a man apparently happy to paddle around in this dark, watery grave. It was tough to shift the mental image of me back then, stewing in a pool of coal smut and separated, decaying flesh, surrounded by the cloud of the flies that feasted upon it. Tougher still was the realisation that, faced with the same set of circumstances, the news of what was in the water probably wouldn't have deterred me from jumping in.

After I moved to Manchester and started a family, I became more sensible where water was concerned. While in the heart of the city I still felt the pull to water, but I'd gained a level of control by then. In Salford, where I have worked for the last twenty years, I have the River Irwell, the wetlands and the ship canal with its own rumoured serial killer. A prowler named The Pusher, who is said to lurk around the towpath waiting for his moment to shove vulnerable men into the grim and greasy waters, where they drown and tumble along in strong currents with all the other water detritus until they're snagged and collected by litter-picking boats. Again, this didn't entirely put me off wanting to risk a swim but my distance from the East Yorkshire coast helped me realise that what I really wanted was the North Sea. Anything else was just a stand-in.

For several years after leaving Withernsea, my visits back home would become less frequent. I had distracting work commitments to contend with and fewer opportunities to head to Yorkshire. When I did go back, my trips were brief, and I had little time to make the sea my focus. I'd tour around town, catching up with the different members of my family then get in the car and head back to Manchester. But when I was there the sea was always a distraction. I'd savour the smell of it that lingered in the air and would often treat myself to a drive along the seafront before leaving town, the way an obsessive ex would take regular journeys past a former girlfriend's house.

In Manchester, whenever I sat down to write, I found that my words always flowed the best while listening to recordings on Spotify of lapping waters and waves crashing. Generic tracks with titles like 'Ocean Meditation Sounds' and 'Fancy Round the World Cruise'. Still, none of them sounded like the North Sea. I could listen to the shuffle of ebbing tides raking pebble beaches and lazy waves sucking at deep rock pools, but they could've been recorded in Margate or the coast of Equatorial Guinea for all I knew. They definitely weren't from the Yorkshire coast, which made a comforting yet moodily complaining sound. One that I held in my head, a sense memory I could feel. After a period of searching, I eventually came across a short field recording of Whitby from 1958, which I listened to on repeat while I tapped at my keyboard. It sounded right for the most part, the screech of the gulls was familiar, the peculiarly brutal wind that slapped the waves into the north-east coastline. But it still wasn't right, the sounds punctuated by the out-of-place put-puts of ancient diesel tugs. These bygone sounds and the knowledge that every bird on the recording had died more than half a century ago ruined the illusion that I was listening to the place that I still considered my home.

When I got a call from my mother and learned that Robert had been hospitalised after he was stung on the foot by a weever fish while paddling at my old south Withernsea swimming spot, I found that I was jealous. *That was my beach*, I thought. *Where things happened to me.* I felt possessively bonded to it in a way that some people feel when an old flame finds someone new, and they are forced to watch their ex enjoying a life they're no longer part of. I've never been like that with people, but I felt it about Withernsea beach. That should have been my foot, my agony, my story to tell. I should have been in a hospital bed, yelling with agony and pressing the nurse alert button to summon more medication, not Robert. I knew that I had no right to feel this way. I'd left town and had flings with other bodies of water, but it was clear that I hadn't moved on. The North Sea was the real thing, my true love, and I wanted us to try again.

*

Effie and I grabbed our things from the car and headed down the old concrete steps, dumping our bags in a sheltered place near the rock wall. She armed herself with her fishing net and bucket and I led her across the sun-warmed sands.

We spent an hour or so hopping between pools and digging our hands into the heavy, squelching sand to wrench out interesting stones and crack them with a hammer, hopeful of a dinosaur tooth but never finding so much as an ammonite. Then the clouds closed in, blocking the sun, and the changed light painted everything with a blueish, gloomy caste. The warmth of the sun disappeared as if a switch had been flipped and Effie immediately began to flag, our golden seaside adventure now resembling a realist movie about coastal deprivation and false hope.

'Look! A fish!' I called out excitably, trying to revive her interest. I pointed out a tiny, sand-skipping creature that looked as if it had just been coughed up by a heavy smoker. She obligingly scooped it into her bucket where it plopped down along with a dozen turd-brown pebbles and a collection of seagull-rended crab limbs.

'No,' I said, my tone brisk and joylessly educational. 'You need to leave it where it was. When the tide comes back in it'll swim away.'

This was the last harsh her mellow could take.

'I'm cold,' she said, as she flicked the fish back onto the sands with her spade, shivering and mournful, her fair skin almost translucent. She looked like an image on a campaign poster highlighting child neglect.

'You said we'd be getting fish and chips,' she said, sourly.

'This is better than fish and chips.'

At this, she turned away and began moodily picking her way back to her towel, where it was warm and didn't smell quite so much like an abandoned fish market.

'Do you want to swim?' I asked, calling to her back, and she responded with the kind of disgusted grunt I'd have expected to have heard if I'd just asked her to eat the contents of her bucket.

'Well, do you mind if I do?'

She knew that I already had my trunks on under my jeans and that any answer she gave me would not only be a cruelty, it wouldn't make a difference. So, she watched in bemusement as I peeled off my clothes and bounded off into the water.

My behaviour was partly down to bottled-up enthusiasm, but it was also for her benefit. I wanted her to see that it was safe and fun but also that I wasn't upset by her lack of interest, even though, of course, I was. At the very least I wanted her to understand my relationship with the sea, and more than that, I wanted her to know it was there for her, just as it had been there for me. But it seemed to Effie, having seen what was left behind on the sands when the tide went out, the wriggling phlegm-like fish and scuttling crustaceans, the many dead and reeking things, that her father was willingly swimming in cold fish soup.

'You're nuts,' she shouted to me, tugging her towel over her head like a hood as she watched me rubbing cold water over my torso. She cracked the spine of a Harry Potter and settled in to read.

'Come in,' I called to her. 'It's warm.'

'Ha!' she said dismissively, watching the breath spewing from my mouth like the vapour from a freshly boiled kettle. But I'd meant it. When the clouds drew back and allowed the sun to warm the water it felt, to me at least, like a bath. She was missing out but I wasn't going to fight it, so I laid back in the sea, trying to lock in with the gentle pulse of the waves. More interested in being part of the habitat. Lying like a small island of seaweed or a lump of driftwood baking in the sun, I half hoped that a seabird would land on me, and I thought of this as saltwater filled my ears with that familiar slurp and I floated free.

I'm not sure how long I was out there, maybe five minutes, maybe half an hour, but I became aware of muffled shouting and raised my head towards the beach. Effie stood at the edge of the shallows, calling out to me. I righted myself and shook the water from my ears, feeling the rush of clear, unmuffled sound.

'Sorry?' I said.

'When are we getting chips?' she called out, skipping backwards as the foam of a breaking wave licked at her feet.

'Just five more minutes!' I lied.

She regarded me moodily then headed back to her book and her towel. It was clear that this was not the fun I had promised her. It wasn't fish and chips or ice cream. Not sculptures and Jurassic adventures on warm sands. It was organised misery. After all of my big talk about this place, I had a sold her a bum deal, her view entirely unpalatable. I could have pointed out to her that some people would dignify my behaviour as 'wild swimming', a hobby where nature enthusiasts gain pleasure from plunging themselves into raw and untampered waters before stopping to post vibrant, ruddy-cheeked selfies on social media. An activity that exists in the hinterland between paganism and Instagram. But Effie had already filed my obsession as a defect and nothing could be done to change her mind. To her the beach looked like one big coffee stain, the waves on the shore like dishwater and, beyond the beach line, stretching out into the distance, the sea as dark and oily as sealskin. And there was her father in the centre of it all. This sad, pale sea creature, churning up the water, too simple to be aware of how miserable his idea of pleasure was. But she had a book and her good sense, so she settled in to read, her own solace and sanctuary, periodically looking up to make sure I hadn't drowned.

While she didn't understand it herself, she knew that if I was in the water I was content. But I also know that she worried. Was concerned that if she took her eyes off me for too long, became engrossed in a wizard duel and left me to my own devices, then I could get lost in a daydream, drift off over the horizon and shrink from her sight forever. But if she did lose me to this sea and was confronted by well-wishers at my funeral, she would at least be able to say, with both bafflement and certainty, 'It's what he would have wanted.'

# Save Burlesque 'til Last

My mother and I were having one of our phone calls.

'I've lost too much weight now,' she told me. 'My bum's whittled down to a point and my tits are just ... what's the word? Flaps!'

It wasn't so much her weight loss she was bothered about, it's that it was affecting her business. For the last few years, she's been working as a semi-professional burlesque dancer and curves are part of her uniform. But she'd been dieting, aiming to alleviate the pressure on her failing knees, and this had cost her her money-maker.

'I need a bum,' she said. 'I need tits. I've got nothing left to wiggle anymore!'

'Maybe you could wear a false bum?' I suggested, cradling the phone between my neck and shoulder while I Googled them for her.

We've always made it a regular habit to talk on the phone, but this was the start of 2020 and after my behaviour at Christmas she'd increased the frequency of her calls. Checking in to make sure that I was doing okay. That I was eating. Not standing on the edge of anything. But once we got these formalities out of the way and she was able place a reasonable amount of faith in my commitment to living, she inevitably fell into talking about her burlesque career, which takes up a lot of her time these days. It's at this point that I enjoy our calls the most, allowing myself to relax into them and listen. This hadn't always been the case though: me sitting in my living room, comfortably functioning as a hotline for her professional anxieties. But just as there is a passage of time that comes between war and peace, there is also a period that comes between the discovery of your mother's burlesque career and the act of scouring the internet for her replacement bottom.

When she'd first told me about her new profession back in 2013, I'd found it hard to process. Not because I'm uptight, growing up I was used to seeing my family naked or partially dressed. We'd think nothing of the fact that my elder brother Robert would regularly wander through the house, twirling his penis like a jolly caretaker with a set of keys. So, none of us was alarmed by the occasional sight of our mother's breasts, in the same way that we weren't shocked by the fact that our dog didn't wear underpants. But when she told me that she'd joined The Ruby Red Performers, a mature burlesque troupe in our home-town, and had begun accepting bookings, I didn't know what to think. Outside of the confines of our home, I'd have to consider her body as other people would and the notion made me queasy. I pictured Dita Von Teese reclining in a giant wine glass. Bettie Page kicking her heels on a chaise lounge. My mother in lingerie folding herself up like a pretzel. She was aware of this, not blind to the idea that her son might struggle with the notion of her shaking her rump to the strains of 'Lady Marmalade'.

'It's okay,' she'd said. 'It's not sexy. You won't be able to see my nipples or anything.'

'*Mum …*'

'Or my vagina,' she added, sensing my distress and delighting in it.

'Oh God.'

'Don't bring God into it,' she said. 'Besides, it's nothing he hasn't seen before. He sees everything so he's definitely seen my vagina.'

'Mum ... please stop saying vagina.'

'Okay, I'm sorry,' she said, then hissed under her breath like a defiant child. 'VaginaVaginaVagina.'

I'd long been used to thinking of my mother as a performer and it had always been something I'd admired about her, so it was strange to have it suddenly start bothering me. I have no memories of a time when she wasn't rehearsing for something, reciting lines and belting out showtunes while she prepared family meals or pushed the vacuum around the living room. She appeared in amateur plays, pantomimes, musicals, often favouring comic roles that allowed her to leap from the wings in a crinoline fairy costume and soak up big portions of stage time. So, it really shouldn't have been a surprise to find out that she'd taken up burlesque dancing. And because it has always been my sister Becky's fate to obediently follow our mother onto the stage, it didn't shock me all that much when I learned that she had joined the Ruby Reds as well.

'I think it'll be good for her confidence,' my mother had said. 'She's always been too shy.'

I'd never thought of this as one of Becky's problems. Growing up, her shyness was one of the things I'd liked the most about her, because I'd always believed it united us. While there are eight years between us in age, it felt like that gap was closed by our mutual fear of becoming the centre of attention. Silent, our heads down, arms pulled in against our torsos, we could make ourselves invisible in social situations, as if we were attending a costume party dressed as the counterpoint to flamboyancy. But now, not only did I have to get my head around the idea that my mother was working the East Yorkshire club circuit and seductively removing her clothes for money, I'd also have to consider that my sister was doing it as well. And not brashly, I imagined, not boldly and confidently, but uncomfortably. Shyly.

I suspected there was something else going on that was beyond building confidence. Of all of us kids, it was Becky who had perhaps been hit the hardest by Robert's death. While my younger brother Ben and I burrowed away into silence and distracting pursuits, it seemed for a while that Becky was spinning off into her own orbit. Untethered, unable to fully relate to a life without Robert in it. I struggled to reach out to her, aware that I might say the wrong thing, knowing that I absolutely would. I also knew that burlesque had helped my mother a lot after Robert died, allowing her to focus on the future by engaging with something new and totally unrelated to a world that he was part of. So, she reached out to Becky, and pulled her in.

'She loves it,' my mother said, but I struggled to buy that, thinking of a younger Becky, confused yet unquestioning as she struggled into her half of a conjoined twin costume for a performance of Aladdin. But I got some small comfort from the knowledge that they'd both be using stage names.

'Mine is Kitty Van Fazz,' she said. 'And Becky's is Crystal Tipps.'

That Becky had a persona to hide behind was a dissociative move that likely worked for the both of us. People would not be staring at my sister's body, I told myself; they'd be staring at Crystal's and while this wasn't ideal, it was just the sort of mental smoke and mirrors I needed.

'Why do you care what they do with their bodies?' my friend Anna had said, when she came over for coffee and I told her how I was feeling. She smirked and punched me on the shoulder. 'You're a bad feminist.'

This put me on the back foot. While I knew that she was needling me for sport, it got under my skin. I had a certain idea of myself, as someone open-minded and accepting, and this didn't fit it. Most of my friends are women and I'd sleep-walked into the notion that this had given me a privileged level of understanding when it came to the female experience. I enjoyed hearing women's dirty jokes, them laughing about who they were sleeping with, their stories about their experiences. They'd often tell me that I wasn't like other men, and I took that to mean that I wasn't like a man at all. That I was somehow special and different. One of them. Then two generations of women in my immediate family started having a great time touring the clubs in their underwear and I'd decided to be a precious little dickhead about it, grasping for coping mechanisms. Proving that I wasn't so very different at all.

'I don't know,' I said. 'It makes me feel weird. I think I just don't want people looking at their bums.'

'But you look at women's bums all the time!'

'Not *all* the time.'

'That's not my point,' Anna said, picking up her coffee cup then quickly putting it down again. 'You don't get to decide when, where and how a woman's bum is acceptable. Be supportive and shut the fuck up.'

I got defensive then, tried to make my stance noble.

'I'm worried about people making fun of them,' I said.

Anna saw through this immediately.

'They don't seem worried,' she said. 'So, are you worried about people making fun of them, or of people making fun of you because they're doing it?'

I tried to reply but it just came out as air. A little steam. I was annoyed because she'd got my number, and so easily too. I knew that it was largely me I was worried about and felt a sense of shame sink into my system. She spotted this and nudged my shin with her toe, sympathetic then.

'Don't feel bad about it,' she said. 'You're a man, most of you need it pointing out to you when you're being an arsehole.'

Up until that point, I'd treated the Ruby Reds act like an anecdote. An icebreaker. Stuck in an awkward silence with someone at a party, I could always dole out that my mother was a burlesque dancer, then double down by mentioning that my sister was one too. I would then either end up in a fun conversation or the person involved in the awkward silence would make their excuses and find someone else to talk to. Either way, my problem was solved. But behind all that was the fact that I'd found a way to pull the focus onto me. I'd recognised that their dancing had value and by framing it as my story I had control over how I got to feel about it. And now I was being called out on that.

'Am I an arsehole?' I asked Anna.

'Oh, honey,' she said gently, finally lifting her cup to her lips. 'You all are.'

I need these kinds of slaps from my friends every so often. To knock off my blinkers. Sometimes I can stop myself from seeing the right path. I worry too much and miss out on things that I could enjoy. In this instance, that my mother and sister were doing something rare and fun. So, I decided to be supportive and shut the fuck up.

This turned out to be much easier than I'd expected. Once I'd given myself over to fully supporting them, I would begin to look forward to my mother phoning up with Ruby Reds tales. Hearing about the odd little venues they'd performed in. The on-stage clothing mishaps and the payment wrangles they'd had with promoters as they'd toured Hull and the Holderness coast. I was aware that living in Manchester made it easier for me to adjust to their career. I wasn't around them and hadn't seen their act, so it remained intangible. It was all audio description for me, a radio play performed down a telephone. They may as well have been working as rodeo clowns for all the difference it made. Then my mother sent me a direct message on Facebook, announcing that things were about to change.

'It's a secret, so you can't tell anyone,' she wrote, her words reading like a conspiratorial whisper. 'But we're going to be on *Britain's Got Talent.*'

My mother has never been able to keep a juicy secret from me but seemed to particularly revel in this one because the stakes were so high.

'Seriously, keep it to yourself. If anyone finds out, we could be pulled from the show.'

This was a lot to take in because there was more than just one concern now. That I would finally end up seeing their act was by far the least of them, replaced by the greater issue that millions of people would. And those people had social media. My mother and sister would be commented upon. Scrutinised. Hashtagged. Memed. And bigger than that, bigger even than the life-changing prize money, was that this was TV and for my family, there was nothing more important.

Growing up in our house, the blare of our TV set was a reliable constant. Often it would broadcast to no one, chatting away to an empty living room like a forgotten elderly relative, but still it remained as necessary to our family's existence as breathing. I woke each morning to the sound of Ben watching cartoons downstairs and nodded off each night to the bassy murmur of my parents cranking the volume of post-watershed crime dramas. I've had it pointed out to me that this is what proves our family was working class, though I never thought of us that way. All I knew for certain was that we were TV class, and that it had long been my mother's fantasy to be on it, looking out at us.

She'd often pick out people on screen and announce her intentions to be one of their number. They might be a market trader on *EastEnders* or a woman in a Coca Cola advert. 'That's going to be me one day,' she'd say, all steel and determination. 'No seriously, it's going to happen.'

It was never her habit to show an interest in lead parts. She had no real aspirations to occupy a starring role, she just wanted to see herself on the screen. Once or twice, she'd tried to make it happen. When regional news crews would arrive to cover an event in our town, she would shimmy into crowd shots and crane her neck, eager to get into the frame. One time she auditioned for the quiz show *Lucky Ladders* but returned from the studio in London downcast and carrying her consolation prize in her purse – a biro bearing the show's logo.

'They told me they liked me,' she said. 'I just wasn't fast enough on the buzzer.'

But now she was going to be hitting primetime and it was my responsibility to ensure that happened. So, I kept quiet. The information about their appearance carbonating inside me during the months leading up to the broadcast, fearful that one wrong word from me and my mother's TV dream would be over. I couldn't risk that, not when she saw it as her reward for years of commitment to cosmic ordering: the practice of submitting your wishes to the universe and waiting for them to be granted.

'I've wanted to be on TV for years,' she said. 'And now it's happening. It really works.'

She saw the appearance on *Britain's Got Talent* as proof positive that her persistent pleas had finally convinced fate to capitulate. But it's odd to me, this insistence that she is not responsible for her own achievements. For my mother, the world shimmers with a magic that powers everything and she's happier to give it thanks than credit her own drive and determination. Ley lines lace her globe, crystals throb with energy; there are fairies at the bottom of the garden and guardian angels overhead, flapping about amongst clouds of pending universal orders. She doesn't question why the universe waited until she was in her sixties to answer her calls, believing that there must have been more pressing requests. But she had faith that her time would come eventually and until then she was happy to wait in the wings, patiently clutching her tap shoes and stretching out her hamstrings. It's obvious to me now that simply having the guts to step out onto a stage and, by her actions say 'This is my sixty-five-year-old body, these are my sixty-five-year-old tits and you are going to watch me do the fucking can-can!' is a magic all of its own. But I don't like to challenge a set of beliefs that make her happy. So, when she talks about things like this, I keep my mouth shut, wary of angering my mother and the universe that has her back.

The day their audition aired, I itched with nerves and anticipation. I switched on ITV and settled down on the sofa but found that I couldn't rest. I kept getting up and leaving the room to pace around. Coming back, sitting down, shoving snacks into my mouth in an effort to stifle my apprehension. I suffered through the other acts, not good or bad, just not my mother and sister, so an aggravation. An unreasonable delay.

Then finally there they were, walking out onto the stage dressed as cleaning ladies, their hair in curlers and scarves. My mother stepped up to the mic to speak and I froze. Held my breath.

'We're from Withernsea, in East Yorkshire,' she said. 'A little seaside town.'

I wasn't used to hearing my hometown being referred to on the TV and I felt that strange kind of conferred pride that you get when your town is known for something even though you had nothing to do with it. A kind of pocket-sized patriotism. But I felt another sensation too, the sickly form of self-consciousness and embarrassment I'd get as a teenager when one of my parents would talk to my friends. But this time my 'friends' were Simon Cowell and an estimated viewing audience of ten million people. I pulled my knees up to my chest, holding myself in a preparatory wince as the ladies lined up and began to perform a ramshackle dance to Queen's 'I Want to Break Free'. A trick to lull the audience into underestimating them, so that they would be even more shocked when the real act began.

I've watched this performance back so often that at the time of writing I could probably do it myself, but first time around it was a blur. Of a dozen middle-aged women brashly peeling off layers of clothing and falling into a synchronised routine. My mother front and centre, my sister off to one side, both of them high kicking, gyrating. Headscarves, bloomers and nighties went flying through the air as they all undressed, until finally there they all were, down to their underwear, my mother at the centre. Chest bouncing. Tassels twirling. It was closer to a saucy seaside postcard made flesh than a Moulin Rouge routine, not what I'd expected at all. There were hip thrusts and suggestive pouts but, true to my mother's word, there were no nipples. No vaginas. Not sexy or anything. Just boldly and defiantly unafraid.

Because the auditions were pre-recorded, I already knew that the Ruby Reds were going through, yet still I got caught up in the tension and peril. 'Wanker,' I spat, as Simon Cowell rolled his eyes and pressed the buzzer to reject them just a few seconds into their performance. When someone crosses me, I like to imagine that I'm the sole witness to seeing them fall down an open manhole, so I can walk away and tell no one about it. I was just picturing this happening to Cowell when he changed his mind and agreed with the other judges, giving the Ruby Reds a fourth yes, putting them through to the live semi-finals and forcing me to mentally reach down into the manhole and offer him my hand.

As the audience cheered, I stood up and found that I was moving towards the TV set, trying to get closer to what I was seeing. My mother told me that this was something she'd often done as a kid when John Lennon appeared on the television. She'd adored him and was so desperate to be in his presence that she'd press her face against the screen and cry with longing, the closeness reducing his image to a black and white grain turned fractal by her tears. But seeing my mother and sister, I didn't want to cry. I think what I wanted was to hug them both, because they had made it. Not in the sense of fame and success, but that they'd got there. They'd made it onto the TV.

'Don't look at Twitter,' my friend John warned me, messaging a few seconds after the broadcast had ended.

'I already have,' I replied, scrolling through the #BGT feed.

'Oh shit,' he said.

'No,' I told him. 'It's mostly nice. It's weird, Twitter is being nice.'

Few people were being cruel or talking about aged bums. Instead, they were talking about body confidence and female empowerment and all the things I should have been thinking about when I was busy thinking about me. My @ replies were full of people telling me that my mother was wonderful.

'I know,' I typed in reply to each, over and over. 'I know. She really is.'

A YouTube clip of their performance went viral, then the press attention began and I learned that my mother was going to be interviewed on the daytime TV show *This Morning*. I struggled to process that this was actually happening. That she was going to appear on a show that I'd watched since childhood and would be sitting on the sofa where famous people had sat before. The Spice Girls. Brian Blessed. Princess Diana's butler. And now my mother. On the TV. In the TV. When I sat down to watch the interview, part of me short-circuited at the sight of it and I can only remember it now in blinks and soundbites.

'Withernsea,' said Philip Schofield.

'Burlesque,' said Amanda Holden, posing with a set of my mother's Union-flag nipple tassels.

'My daughter does it as well,' said my mother, keen to make sure that Becky didn't miss out on the recognition. And as she was asked another question, I thought I saw her resist the temptation to turn to face the camera. To look out at me and wave.

'I knew you were watching,' she told me later.

'How?'

'Because Uri Geller sat on that sofa once.'

In the build-up to their appearance in the semi-finals, Withernsea briefly found itself basking in the glow of a positive media spotlight. ITV sent over a film crew, who plastered the Ruby Reds in make-up and filmed them browsing in quaint shops then sassing their way along the beach to the strains of 'I'm Every Woman'. They were made up to look like the cast of *Calendar Girls* and were interviewed wearing tea-dresses and sitting around a gingham-laid café table, candy-coloured bunting threaded across the trees behind them. It pleased me to see the town like this. Captured flatteringly in well-chosen angles, made to seem genteel. As being close to its mid-century heyday. This was Withernsea in its Sunday best, chest proudly out. Dressed up for the nation.

In the meantime, the Ruby Reds had been working with a choreographer and his impact was immediately noticeable. Not least because, for the semi-final routine, the women would each be fitted with an exploding bra. My mother made sure to warn me about this part beforehand, anticipating how I'd react.

'I know you'll worry but don't, it's totally safe,' she told me. 'They're using Lady Gaga's people.'

By the time their performance rolled around I was so used to seeing them in their underwear that it seemed odd to think that I'd ever worried about it. So, free from discomfort and only concerned with the notion that they might reach the final, I watched them dance to 'Fat Bottomed Girls' and 'Are You Gonna Be My Girl?' while dressed as crossing guards. I watched them strip down. I watched my mother hurtle across the stage on a gold scooter. And then I watched hers and Becky's breasts explode in six-foot jets of pyrotechnic flame. As the fires died out and the audience cheered, Becky blew the smoke from her steel teats as if she were casually extinguishing the candles on a birthday cake. To me, this looked like the action of a confident winner but as it was, the public vote placed them last, though by that by that point it didn't matter. They'd already scored an agent and the opening slot at Hull Pride. At an age when most people were slowing down, they were just getting started.

In the afterglow of primetime fame, the Ruby Reds picked up a lot of bookings. They appeared at biker festivals, in a Sainsbury's ad, featured on Channel 5's *Up Late with Rylan* and were invited to take up a residency at a casino in the Black Sea resort of Batumi. Though one booking in particular left my mother considerably excited.

'We're going to be dancing on a cruise ship in October,' she told me, before checking herself and dialling down her statement. 'Well, I say cruise ship. It's the Hull to Rotterdam ferry.'

But ferry or otherwise, it represented performance on the high seas and the very concept made her giddy.

'I've always wanted to dance on a ship,' she said. 'So, I asked the universe for it.'

'When?' I asked.

'Oh, I don't know,' she said. 'The sixties? You can't rush the universe.'

The ship was named *The Pride of Rotterdam* and the Ruby Reds had been booked onto it as part of the Hull City of Culture celebrations. I've been on this ship and am familiar with the bar where they were performing. I have sat beside the crescent-shaped stage and the large dance floor in what amounts to a floating casino. It was there that I'd witnessed the house band, churning out covers before a raucous and drunken audience, be accosted by a guy who invaded the stage and tried to snatch the mic from the female singer. As security staff dragged him away, she tried to restart the song and another man shouted at her from the audience.

'Show us your fadge!'

It bothered me to think of my mother and sister dancing there, while drunk people cat-called and tried to involve themselves. But I needed to remember how tough and flinty the two of them have become. That I don't need to protect them. I'd seen and heard that they could handle themselves. So, rather than worry, I now try to enjoy the way they control the space around them. For my mother, this has been to make use of her age, stage managing the people in her vicinity and making them part of her own show. Wherever she went on the ferry, she found that young men would race to help her.

'Mama, let me carry your bags,' they'd say, opening doors for her and offering up their seats. 'After you, Mama.'

There was a time when she would have hated this, to have her seniority highlighted in this way, but aged seventy now, she has learned to appreciate the benefits of deference. Recognised that she wants that kind of help, which at the moment feels more about respect than a suggestion that she is infirm. This has become her role in the troupe, introduced on stage as a great-grandmother and appearing in a glittering gold gown, surrounded by an entourage of twirling, basque-clad dancers as if she were the ageing madam of a bordello. Still, there is mischief and fire in her. The performer's urge to make a show out of everything.

Between sets on the ship, she'd get chatting to passengers and tell extravagant lies about what she did with her life when she wasn't dancing. She has go-to stories that she likes to tell. That she is a retired kickboxer, that she is part of the witness relocation programme, and lately, that she runs a celebrity anal bleaching studio in the Yorkshire Dales.

'I can't tell you,' she replied in hushed tones, when the other passengers speculated about her most famous clients and pressed her for intel. 'I've signed non-disclosure agreements. All I'll say is that I've treated six members of the royal family and that's my final word on the matter.'

She delights in this, another kind of performance. One that subverts people's expectations of her. Seeing what she can get away with. Playing with the trust granted to her by age, though not an age so great that people might immediately consider that she has dementia.

Becky, meanwhile, has become unflappable. Her experience making her bulletproof and determined. If the universe was responsible for bringing the Ruby Reds to the national stage, then it's my sister's drive that has kept them dancing along it, using a power that she didn't have before, or at least one I hadn't realised she'd always had.

A key part of the Ruby Reds' show these days has become Becky's solo spot. Ostensibly it's to necessitate a costume change for the rest of the troupe, who scatter into the wings to frantically rip off their bodices and hoik up new tights. But for me it's a demonstration of the person Becky has grown into. Alone on stage for several minutes, absorbing the full focus of the audience's attention, she acts out the discovery of a rainbow-coloured outfit then excitedly puts it on, piece by piece, to the strains of 'Proud Mary' before beckoning the rest of the ladies out onto the stage and dancing up a sweat that Tina Turner would be proud of. There is nothing uncomfortable or shy about it, no smallness of physicality. It's a showcase of her boldness and confidence and also, of how much I'd got her wrong.

'I was shitting myself beforehand,' she told me after I saw her perform this routine for the first time, at an open-air, 1940s-themed Veteran's Day event in Hull. She was rosy-cheeked and laughing, light-headed from the ridiculous thrill of it. 'When I'm up there though, I love it. I don't give a stuff.'

These days, it's mainly my mother that I worry about. About her knees and the number of falls she's had while doing the can-can, but mostly I worry that she has added fire-eating to her repertoire and is looking at ways to incorporate it into her dance routines. She WhatsApped me clips of her setting her tongue on fire and spitting a plume of flame into the air, then phoned up to detail how she'd managed to burn all of the hair off her forearms.

'I think my biggest problem is going to be fire regulations,' she said contemplatively, and I considered all of the problems that were bigger than fire regulations.

'But couldn't you set your costume on fire?' I asked, picturing her engulfed in flames and thrashing around on the floor while the audience applauded, mistaking it for part of the act.

'Not if I do it naked.'

'Oh God, Mum ...'

I then asked her the question that I often think of when we talk. 'How long can you keep this up?'

'Oh, I'm going to live to be 107,' she replied, referring to a request I know she placed with the universe long ago.

'Oh God ...' I said, feigning shock. Picturing her bursting out of a cake on her 100th birthday or rappelling down from a chandelier on her 105th. But privately I put my faith in the universe too, hopeful for at least another forty years of this.

# The Letting Go

## *Track 1*

The first time I truly saw Alex, he was crouching on the living room floor of a bungalow in the village of Bempton, dropping AA batteries onto the strings of an electric guitar and recording the sounds to a small, portable tape deck. With each drop the strings issued a distressed, resonating clang, fizzing with distortion. The sound was at odds with the environment, where he lived with his grandparents. It ricocheted off the horse brasses on the fireplace and the display cabinet of bone china ornaments before being sucked into the plump, chintzy sofa and disappearing. He looked up at me, a giddy smile on his face.

'Fucking ace!' he said.

'Fucking ace!' I said.

I picked up my bass guitar and ground the strings into my amp, turning the treble setting down to one and the bass setting up to ten. It let out a low, gut-disturbing moan that descended into a distressed clarinet-like squall. Most people would hear a noise like this and fear that, somewhere, a baby was trapped. But Alex and I were operating on a different frequency.

'It sounds like jazz,' I said.

'Yeah!' Alex said, then picked up his guitar and played the one chord he could competently hold, over and over, while I mashed the bass strings and the windows shuddered.

Ning ning ning. Honk honk honk. Drone. Squeal.

If anyone with a generous heart was listening to us they might have favourably compared our music to the sound of a clown car ploughing into a horse. Others might have heard the hiss of John Coltrane's ghost seething with outrage. But to us it felt like new sonic frontiers. We were impatient to finish playing so we could listen back to the recording and revel in our work but we also never wanted it to stop. We looked at each other and locked eyes, unable to suppress our smiles. We were falling in love with the sound we were making and, it felt, a little with each other. It seemed to us like we were inventing a language that no one else understood at that point, but would come to and, when they did, they would value it. We heard magic and meaning in these screeches and howls, even as our eardrums turned to pâté.

'Fucking ace!' Alex shouted. And it was.

Seeing someone for the first time isn't the same thing as laying eyes on them. Alex and I had actually done that a few months earlier at the start of term, when we'd both signed up for an art course at Hull College in 1993. It would take me another week or so to build up the confidence to speak to him and a further few months before, drunk on noise in a pensioner's bungalow, I would finally see him. As an ally, a brother and a rock that I could tether myself to.

## Track 2

When I was born, my father had seen great potential in me, hopeful that I might one day become British tennis No.1 or follow in my grandfather's footsteps and join the RAF. But it was soon clear to him that I possessed no physical gifts, no dynamism. I got breathless while eating. Ran as if I was being divebombed by bees, my arms bonelessly flailing. My childhood was notable not for my successes but for the catalogue of injuries that my lack of co-ordination had gifted me. When

I slipped at a fairground while racing towards a hotdog stand and collided with the condiment shelf, breaking both my nose and a box containing miniature wooden forks, my father had long since reached the point where that sort of thing had become painfully typical.

'God,' he'd said, helping me up off the ground. 'It's like you're part clown.'

Thinking of myself back then, with my beet-red nose and my early-blooming size twelve feet, I get the sense that I was just one balloon animal away from my father handing me over to a circus. And had he done that, it would have been a mercy. Saving me from high school, where I would learn to become profoundly embarrassed about everything I did and said and, over time, would begin to wonder if it would be better for everyone if I quietly and discreetly crawled away and died. So, when it was announced that our family was moving to Withernsea I was immediately hungry for it, a rare instance of me being able to both recognise the necessity of something and demonstrate the wherewithal to capitalise on my circumstances. I saw our journey north for what it was: a reset button and an opportunity to start afresh, where no one was aware of me or my past. It seemed to me that, by starting over again in Withernsea, I would be able enjoy the upside of killing myself without the inconvenience of having to die.

Before we even made the move north, I began work on my backstory. I already knew that I would be starting college in Hull a few months after we moved, and I wanted to be fully prepared. To have my transformation complete and comfortably bedded in before my first day on campus. I wouldn't actively present a false narrative as such but, if pressed, I was fully prepared to lie with my hand on a bible. I had never tasted alcohol at that point but if someone asked me what my favourite drink was, I would say that it was Jack Daniels and that I liked it very much. *Can I play guitar?* '*Why, yes,*' I'd say. '*Yes, I can.*' Then privately, desperately, learn. If offered a cigarette, I'd mime smoking, just like I did with the candy ones when I was seven, hoping that I wouldn't disgrace myself by trying to light the filter. This kind of scripting was essential to my plan and in preparation for fielding the more difficult questions I expected to face, I'd stand before the bathroom mirror, interrogating my reflection.

'Are you a virgin?' I asked myself.

'No!' I replied, trying not to sound too defensive. Analysing the evasive flitting of my eyes. I tried again but reduced the note of alarm in my voice.

'No.'

Again, but more casual.

'No?'

I still sounded too uncertain, like something bad had happened to me but I wasn't sure if it counted as sex. Again, an octave lower.

'NO.'

The visual identity I presented was arguably my biggest hurdle. Aware that there was no second chance to make a first impression, and that mistakes came with genuine consequences, I had to get it right. This involved being brutally and ruthlessly honest with myself. So, I set about writing a list of my physical faults and flaws. The things I wanted, needed, to fix and how I'd go about that.

| | |
|---|---|
| **Problem**: Legs too short, out of proportion with torso. | **Solution**: Buy tight jeans, Dr Marten boots. |
| **Problem**: Torso is skinny but doughy. No abs. | **Solution**: Sit ups. Swim in sea. |
| **Problem**: Arms have no muscle definition. | **Solution**: Press ups. Swim in sea. |
| **Problem**: Face too long, lolling mouth. | **Solution**: Try to breathe through nose more. Grow goatee. |
| **Problem**: Hair not long enough, not cool. | **Solution**: Grow hair very long. |
| **Problem**: Feet too big. | **Solution**: Use as talking point. |

It seemed to me, that if I made enough drastic changes to myself and presented a diverting image then people would draw their own flattering conclusions about me and not stop to wonder if I knew what it was like to kiss a girl. So, I treated my self-analysis like a science, studying areas of improvement with a greater level of intensity and commitment than I'd ever applied to my GCSEs. It didn't take me long to realise that building a new version of myself from the ground up was a mammoth task and would take more time than I really had. What I needed was an off-the-rack identity that I could grow into once I'd settled in up north, so I decided to steal one.

The logical choice was to emulate my elder brother Robert, who ticked most of the boxes for what I considered to be cool and appealing. He smoked. Played electric guitar. Wore a black leather jacket and had fallen into the habit of starting each day by snorting speed off a saw-backed hunting knife before jumping on his motorbike and riding to work. I only got so far as the leather jacket before losing my nerve about the rest. It was clear that if I was going to find a new identity, I'd need to broaden the net.

Watching TV with my family, I took to sizing up movie characters that I found appealing and discreetly making notes about them on an A4 notepad. I listed their attributes, their pros and cons, applying the same rigour that I applied to myself. Over time I built up a sizable dossier, containing the assessed merits of actors like John Cusack in *The Sure Thing*, Harrison Ford in *The Temple of Doom* and Eddie Murphy in *Beverley Hills Cop*. Each of them put through my scoring matrix.

'What are you doing?' my father asked me one evening, nodding to my pad.

'Homework,' I replied, then applied a nine out of ten hair thickness rating to Patrick Swayze.

'I thought you'd finished school?'

'This is for the start of college,' I said, and my answer seemed to satisfy him. His finally studious son, diligently rating Hollywood actors by height, charisma and sex appeal.

As our moving date approached I considered this body of research, these score sheets and reams of frenzied annotation, then dismissed it all. None of the pages contained an answer that worked for me. Every option fell down on my inability to handle a whip, wisecrack my way out of peril or hold a woman above my head. I felt sure, though, that a new me was out there, waiting to be selected. And though it took me a while to realise, I'd already been preparing my new identity for some time. The problem was, I was too busy framing it as a troubling obsession.

## Track 3

The year before I moved to Withernsea I fell in love with Steven Tyler, the lead singer of the band Aerosmith. 'In love' isn't the right term really. It's not like I wanted to go to bed with him. I had no fantasies about us one day shopping for mid-century furniture together. But I found him alluring in a way I couldn't fully articulate at the time. I'd never felt this way about another man before, so 'in love' was how I saw it.

My interest in him began after reading a magazine interview with Janet Jackson in which she'd described Tyler as one of the most attractive men alive, and, looking at the accompanying photo of him, I found myself agreeing. His sassy confidence while wearing leggings, that sink plunger pout. Not handsome but appealing in a way that made handsomeness seem like a trinket. Something commonplace that most people could achieve pretty easily with some dental work and a decent haircut. Wanting more, I bought an Aerosmith album with a photo of two trucks having sex on the cover and found that I was in love with Tyler's music too. Pretty soon I was spending all of my money on Aerosmith records and clipping photos of the band from magazines to tack onto my bedroom wall, converting it into what qualified, depending on your perspective, as either a shrine or a stalker's lair. Lying in bed and listening to Tyler's alley cat voice singing 'Sweet Emotion', no direction I could look without seeing his face staring back at me, I felt closer to the world he inhabited. An appealing one, where the letter G was surplus. Full of struttin' and rockin' and lovin'. These were distant, exciting things that I dearly wanted for myself and he seemed to have in abundance.

I recorded Aerosmith's appearances on MTV, building up a VHS archive that I re-watched analytically, studying Steven

Tyler's form. I made note of the way he draped his body in diaphanous fabrics and long, technicolour silks, which followed the movement of his limbs like comic book motion lines as he pranced across the stage or confidently humped his mic stand. Of how, though he moved like a first-year drama student playing a wood nymph, all strange, elongated arm movements, reckless twirls and ants-in-pants shimmies, he somehow didn't seem ridiculous. It would eventually dawn on me that what I needed was to transform myself into someone like him. If I could adopt just a pinch of his energy and self-assurance, then the things I wanted for my new life in the north, to be seen, respected and desired, to not be thought of as a clown, would fall into place. And if I was very, very lucky, then Janet Jackson might want to kiss me.

When we made the move to Withernsea, I carefully packed up and transported my shrine, which I reassembled in my new bedroom then expanded upon, drawing a life-size mural on my wall of Aerosmith's lead guitarist Joe Perry copied from a photo of him performing at a huge stadium concert in California. I drew the crowds beyond him, the thousands of small, cheering faces, a wall of adoration. And here I would mime along to 'Walk this Way' or 'Love in an Elevator' – twirlin', struttin' and bein' Steven Tyler. While I was imitating him, I'd forget my own appearance and think of the two of us as physically identical, but once I was done and the dizziness had passed, I'd remember that there were horses who bore a closer resemblance to Steven Tyler than I did. Put one in a Lycra jumpsuit and a headscarf and I wasn't even a close second. But I didn't see this as an obstacle. While I knew that transforming myself into his doppelgänger represented a challenge, I believed that time and determination could get me anywhere, and that it all came down to the lips.

I'd read about the legend of Milo of Croton, a sixth-century Greek wrestler, who was said to have picked up a new-born calf and continued to do so every day until he was able to lift the adult bull it became. Inspired by his dedication, I spent my first summer in Withernsea performing daily mouth-stretching exercises in front of the mirror, opening my jaws as far as they would allow out of the hope that, in time, my mouth would become as broad and flapping as Tyler's. I'd daydream about developing an anaphylactic reaction so drastic that it would permanently puff up my lips, leaving them as plump and kissable as his. But lacking a nut allergy or easy access to a hornet's nest, I got by on gently blowing while pouting.

'Why do you keep sighing?' my mother asked, looking up from the TV as I pout-puffed my way through the living room. 'Are you depressed?'

'No,' I replied, caught out and embarrassed, not willing to admit to her how deeply I wanted to transform myself into someone else. 'I'm fine.'

'Well, whatever it is you're up to, stop it. You sound like a sad little train.'

I ignored her and carried on, like *The Little Engine That Could*. Later that summer I bought some tight jeans and a few flowing shirts from a charity shop. I started wearing an amethyst pendant and let my hair grow out into the establishing phases of what would become a billowing mullet. If my aim had been to dress as if I was having an early-onset midlife crisis, then I was nailing it but by the time I started college that September. I had high hopes for me and my new look. While I was still shy and insecure, I was also convinced that people would notice me in a way they hadn't in Suffolk. That, after all the work I'd put in, they'd find me impressive and alluring, allowing me to ride the wave of their assumptions until the fantasy became inseparable from the reality.

My mind moved to that scene in *Grease 2*, when the dorky Maxwell Caulfield appears on his motorbike at a roadside bowling alley, his true identity concealed by black leather and sunglasses. Mouths drop open in awe and the cast is driven to launch into a song called 'Who's That Guy?'. Each of them curious about this new and mysterious arrival.

On my first day at college though, my new look went without comment. It was the same the next day, and the one after that. No one stopped to ask me what I drank or if I'd convinced anyone to have sex with me. While I'd rehearsed them often, my prepared responses went unsaid. After a few weeks spent wafting through the campus, it was clear to me that the chances of anyone thinking to ask who that guy was had moved from slim to improbable. So, I went to my mother for advice.

'I'm not sure this is working,' I said, confessing everything about my efforts to reinvent myself. 'I think I look like a nerd.'

'You are not a nerd!' she said, offended. 'None of my children are nerds.' She looked me up and down. 'You look ... cool.'

She was trying hard to keep the doubt from her voice. This was surely a matter of maternal pride. After all, no one wants to admit that they went to the effort of gestating a baby for nine months only to discover that its life's ambition is to resemble the man who wrote 'Dude (Looks Like a Lady)'. But the evidence in front of her defied even the blindness of a mother's love.

'Okay,' she admitted. 'Maybe you could at least stop wearing that blouse.'

'It's not a blouse,' I said, annoyed. 'It's a shirt.'

'What size is it?'

I pulled at the collar and craned my neck to look at the label.
'I can't see a size,' I said. 'It just says "Petite".'

## Track 4

Recognising a lost cause when it was staring me in the face
I pressed the reset button again, restyling my hair, abandon-
ing my facial stretches and re-donating my blouses to Oxfam.
I reminded myself that you *do* get a second a chance to make
a first impression if no one paid attention to you the first time
around. So, I decided on something less drastic. I enrolled on a
different course and started wearing the kind of plaid shirts and
baggy jeans I'd seen in Nirvana's press photos. I accessorised
my look with an eyeball pendant and a matching leather bracelet, purchased from a shop in Hull named Kathmandu, which
sold whale song CDs and lumps of crystal big enough to club a
man to death with. Still, I knew there was something missing.
An accessory to define me.

'I want to learn guitar,' I told my father, and I could tell
that he was relieved. That I was finally doing something he
approved of.

My father had been obsessed with music since he was a
young boy, amassing a collection of records that would go
on to require their own room and now so densely pack my
parent's loft they likely qualify as insulation. When he wasn't
working his shifts at the British Gas terminal in Easington, he
would sit in the corner of our living room beside the stereo,
a pair of headphones the size of a bisected coconut clamped
over his ears. This seemed as much about shutting us kids out
as it was about letting the music in and it was clear that, with
his headphones on, he entered a different, preferable world. In

the real world someone was always prodding him, badgering him for money or a lift somewhere, but when he eliminated us with music, he became a serene figure of stone. Impenetrable, eyes closed, likely picturing himself watching Elvis Presley in Vegas or Johnny Cash in Folsom prison. Anywhere but our living room.

'I've always felt I had a song in me,' he'd tell me, before being struck with the same lost and distant expression he'd sometimes adopt when trying to remember where he'd put his car keys. But I could tell it was significant for him, that he was thinking of lost opportunities. He'd once gone so far as to buy himself an acoustic guitar and we'd occasionally see him bent over it, plucking at the strings. We would listen to the buzz and thrum of his malformed chords then say, 'That sounds nice,' as if we were praising an ape for passably imitating human behaviour. Being ambidextrous, he could never find a way to string the guitar that felt comfortable for him, so it came to sit in the corner of the spare room, left-hand strung and largely unplayed. Then there I was, ready to pick it up, right-hand string it and fulfil one of his ambitions, believing that somewhere between Joe Perry and my father, there was a space for me.

We couldn't afford lessons, so my father bought me a home tuition video from WHSmith, presented by a man with a rat-tail mullet and a soft, plodding voice, who perched on a stool in a gloomy, otherwise empty studio set, embracing his guitar as if it was a lady he had drugged. There was something about this man that made me feel like I was watching *Before They Were Famous* footage of a now-dead cult leader. But music was the cult I had chosen and despite my reservations about the teacher, I was excited. This was the starting point that would one day surely lead me from a bedroom in Withernsea to a stadium in California.

'This is an E Major chord,' the man said languidly, stroking the curved body of the guitar. 'Practice holding this chord, releasing it then reapplying it. Do this every day for one week.'

I was obedient for a while, spending weeks diligently transitioning between E, A and G chords. But I got impatient, wanting an immediate result, a set of hands that moved like Joe Perry's. Not ones like mine, which clumped along the neck of the guitar as if they were hooves. So, I placed it back in the corner of the spare room and went to my father again.

'I think I'm more of a bassist,' I told him.

'What?' he said, confused and, I could tell, disappointed. 'Why? You can't play songs on a bass.'

Of all the words ending in -ist that I could have chosen to self-identify as, bassist seemed to be the worst. For him, it represented something significant. Or rather, insignificant.

'It's just a rhythm section instrument,' he continued softly, his words fading along with his dreams of my stardom. 'You'll be in the *background*.'

This was an unfamiliar sensation, to have gained his faith for the first time then lost it so quickly, snatching away the pleasing picture he was building of me. I couldn't nail the feeling exactly, which occupied a region somewhere between grief and liberation. But I knew that it was the right decision, that bass would suit me better. It was an instrument that would allow me to be both in the spotlight but also hiding, playing simple notes and finding my feet while I prepared myself for centre stage. My father was resistant for a while but there was something convincing about my mix of determination and defeat, and finally he capitulated.

'Okay,' he said, making a calculation. Dialling his levels of expectation for me back down from Superstar to Clown. 'I suppose it's still music.'

He took me to a pawn shop in Hull where he bought me a black and white Encore bass guitar. I liked the reassuring weight of it, an instrument I could feel safe behind. The strings felt fat and secure when I pressed them into the fret board. And crucially, there were only four of them, which made it an easier job. We took it home and I sat in my bedroom, working my way through a *Bass for Beginners* book, all the while thinking 'you can't play songs on a bass', and that I needed a band.

## Track 5

When Alex and I first encountered each other at college we looked like the results of the same genetic experiment. We each had long features and soft, mousy brown hair. We were tall, skinny and not quite sure how to stand without making it look like labour. But we dressed as if we were from different worlds. Alex, sensibly, in pressed jeans and plain, coloured t-shirts, a ski jacket and the kind of trainers that your dad might wear for jogging. His hair was neatly side-parted and short, while I was growing mine out again into grungy hanks. He looked remarkably out of place in our art studio, so well turned out and presentable in this chaotic room where the walls were papered with abstract nudes and the floor was spattered with drizzles of paint and spilt glue. I looked *slightly* more like I belonged in that room, but I was trying hard to look like I had a right to be there. Flamboyantly sketching with my right arm and posing against an easel with my left, determinedly angling my wrist in an effort to get someone to notice my eyeball bracelet. The only person who did spot it, was Alex.

'Where did you get that?' he said, gesturing to my wrist as he pinned a sheet of paper to his easel.

My initial reaction was to flinch, to fall into the high school fear that I was about to be humiliated and would soon feel the bracelet being wrenched from my arm. But this was what I'd wanted by assembling another new look. Attention. Recognition. So, I went with it.

'Kathmandu,' I told him.

'In Nepal?' he said, seeming impressed.

There was a brief excitement at this point, realising that I could use my unknown status to lie. Tell him that I had been around the world on a voyage of personal discovery. He would be able to picture me having transcendent experiences with orange-robed monks in mountain top temples. In India, laying a garland over a statue of Ganesh. Meditating naked on a rock in the Gulf of Thailand. But I went with honesty.

'No,' I said. 'The shop, near the train station.'

'Oh, right,' he said. 'I've been there. It smells like hippies. What music do you like?'

We went for lunch together that day and from that point on we spent as much time in each other's company as decency would allow, gobbling up every detail of each other's lives in the excitement of newness and sharing. We told each other stories about our lives and experiences, deeply identifying with one another and finding comedy in the smallest of things, laughing until we winced with pain from lack of breath. Over time, our giddiness became our known and shared identity at college. We began to alienate our fellow students, annoying them with our disrupting and increasingly exclusionary sense of humour.

'You two are morons,' a girl named Kath said, when she walked into the studio after lunchbreak to find Alex and I bent double and hysterical in the middle of the room, where we'd discovered a boiled egg resting on the floor without explanation beside a photo of the *EastEnders* actress, Susan Tully. Across the photo, in toothpaste, was written the word 'Lungs'. Someone's absurdist art statement, we assumed, but funnier than either of us could adequately convey.

'You wouldn't … understand,' I managed finally, gasping for air.

'I understand that you two are not right in the head,' Kath replied.

I should have seen Kath's reaction, and the way she relayed this encounter to the other students, as a negative, but instead it made me feel that Alex and I were both on an uncommon wavelength, and this meant we were special. Having worked so hard to find friends, it might seem odd that I would so readily distance myself from other people, but with Alex I had everything I needed.

While apart, we'd often spot things that we knew would amuse the other and try to keep them in our heads until we could share them. And when it came to discovering new music, it was the same kind of process. The only real difference was that with music we took things very seriously. Our evenings were regularly spent playing records to each other down the phone. Songs we'd recorded off the TV or bought in Woolworth's earlier that day.

'Listen to this,' one of us would say, holding the receiver to our speakers or up against the television until the final notes of a song had faded, then we'd clamp the phone back to our ears to ask 'What did you think?'

Our responses to each other were always swift and positive, and it was clear that something special was happening between us. A tuning into each other's tastes. A twinning. I didn't really need to alter myself for Alex because we were changing and building something together; a mutual appreciation of music and art and each other. Over time we would start to dress in the same way, assembling a look we'd approximated from watching MTV's *120 Minutes*. While we'd hoped to be mistaken for members of Dinosaur Jr. we would instead be mistaken for each other. We were a pair, a two-man gang, sleepwalking into an unkempt uniform and also into something else. I was the first to say it.

'I think we should start a band.'

I felt immediately sick, expecting Alex to blurt a laugh and detonate our friendship, but his response was animated and enthusiastic.

'Yes!' he said, and I felt as if I had successfully proposed marriage to someone who'd been waiting for me to pop the question.

Alex bought himself a beaten-up Fender Mustang and the two of us took to our bedrooms, poring over our guitar manuals and sitting in front of *Top of the Pops*. Getting frustrated with the directors' artsy cutaways as we tried to study musician's finger placements on fretboards in an attempt to work out how they made those sounds. After a few weeks of practice, we found that we could each play rudimentary versions of simple, popular songs and were overconfident enough to start writing some of our own.

'I've got this bit that goes dum diddle dee, dum diddle diddle dee,' I told Alex. 'If you played a straight ning ning G over that…'

'Or what if I played neee neeee neee neee?' he replied, a strange see-sawing squeal emitting from the back of his throat.

'Yes!' I said, assembling these pieces in my head and hearing a symphony.

Because we didn't know how to write sheet music, we each wrote down the words 'neee neee neee' and 'dum diddle diddle dee' on lined paper as if we were filling out staves. Then we took to his grandparents' bungalow and shook the windows, falling in love with ourselves and our music. With our jazz. With our new sonic frontiers.

Ning ning ning. Honk honk honk. Drone. Squeal.

## Track 6

Although we had no lyrics and there was only 'dum diddle dee', we were already writing our myth. Making ourselves presentable for the press. We took ourselves down to Withernsea beach with my mother's camera to take some promo shots of us posing beside the crumbling cliffs. On the way, we discussed how we'd market ourselves.

'Maybe we could say we play Grunge Pop?' Alex said, as he scanned the cliff face for a suitable spot for us to stand, his eye pressed against the camera's viewfinder.

'I think we should call it Art Rock,' I said, climbing onto a large dirt clod at the foot of the cliffs. 'Because we're artists,' I added. 'We have our own style, you can't label it.'

I was ignoring the fact that I'd attempted to do just that, and so was Alex, each of us knowing that too much criticism at this early stage would ruin the good time we were having. We also knew that, while we couldn't really play yet and didn't have any conventional songs, we could work on that and, while we did, we could focus on being wild and interesting. What art college had taught us more than anything else was to be cynical. That we could get away with whatever we liked as long as we framed it in the right way. If people told us that they didn't like our music, we could explain to them that they just didn't understand it. That we had our own tuning. That our music was Cubist.

'Art Rock,' Alex said, feeling out the words, giving them air. 'I like it.'

'Me too!' I said, standing on one leg atop the clod, my arms reaching to the sky. 'Quick! Take my picture. I can't hold this for long.'

I found ways to legitimise our position, seeking out music that was chaotic enough for us to emulate. I discovered a band named Doo Rag, who shouted and drummed on cardboard boxes and bin lids while hammering away at steel guitars. I played Alex one of their songs.

'Fucking hell,' he said. 'That's just a noise. We could do that.'

'I know!'

*We could do that.* This was the liberating thing, and the two of us worked to find music that matched and validated our limitations. At the beginning of '94 we discovered a Belgian band named dEUS, who self-identified as film makers rather than musicians. When they toured the UK, we went to see them play and marvelled as their guitarist dropped his instrument and began kicking it across the stage, like a sullen child toeing a tin can down the street. It wailed and clanged, and a light came on in our heads. We went back to our bedrooms and wrote songs for kicked guitar. Songs for out-of-tune instruments. Songs for two-string, one-string and no-string guitars. We made a virtue of our lack of ability, telling ourselves that competency was something that got in the way, stopping us from reaching what really mattered about music. To us, virtuosity was soulless, something akin to maths. We, unable to read music or explain with a gun to our heads what allegro meant, considered ourselves to be free and open, able to reach the raw truth of music because we weren't concerned with the dusty old rulebook.

The gaps in our ability were filled with plans and schemes. We didn't know song structure, but we were art students, and we knew how to make merchandise. When we decided to call our band Ruby Vroom, Alex designed our logo and hand-painted it on a t-shirt above a fleur-de-lys pattern, based on the fabric design of his grandparents' sofa. Beneath it he wrote the words 'Cock in Pocket' in a sloped, drunken font. Then we changed our name to something else. And again. And again. Writing and rewriting the myth, very rarely the music, but always the t-shirt.

When the two of us rehearsed together, we generally spent an hour or so agonising over chords until our fingers locked up or bled, then we'd fall into distractions. Most often these related to how we'd conduct ourselves in interviews. We'd pose each other imagined questions from intrigued journalists and for every question we'd have an evasive response. A Houdini answer designed to avoid the fact that we didn't really under-stand how music worked.

'Who is your biggest musical influence?' I'd ask, adopting the Dutch accent of a VJ on MTV Europe.

'I think it's restrictive to define influence by music alone,' Alex would say. 'I'm influenced by lots of things. Architecture. Horse brasses. The smallpox anti-virus.'

'The smallpox anti-virus?' I'd say, leaning in, pretending to be fascinated by the band and its unconventional creative pro-cess. 'Why?'

'Well, I'd like to answer that question with a question,' Alex would say. 'Why not?'

'The first single on your new album is called "Cock in Pocket," what's it about?'

'What would you like it to be about?' he'd reply. Then we'd flip roles and Alex would quiz me. 'How would you describe your music?'

'It sounds like the sea,' I'd say, looking out of the window for inspiration. 'Like seagulls screeching. Like sandcastles crumbling. Like this …' Then I'd pick up my bass and produce a sound like a traction engine being pushed into a quarry.

The thrill we got from making music in the same room began to be outweighed for me by this sort of thing. The planning. The mapping out of our future in this way, writing the fantasy. I was colouring in the edges, as fascinated by the activity around music as I was by the music itself. I saw our career reaching out ahead of us. We'd top Album of the Year polls in the serious music press, but somehow manage to infiltrate the mainstream as well, breaking into the pop charts by fundamentally redefining the nature of sound. We'd appear on *Top of the Pops*, punching our guitars and screaming local newspaper headlines into a megaphone. Teenage fans would scream for us and bop, waving banners with fan art images of us reimagined as Greek deities. Aspiring musicians would study our finger placements.

'The New Sound We've Been Searching For!' the NME front cover would scream, over an image of our faces artfully shot in grainy black and white on Withernsea beach. A double page centre spread would feature me looking sullen in front of one of my abstract paintings or sculptures, overlaid with an attention-grabbing quote. 'We're at war with mediocrity!'

I spent a good deal of time thinking about how good it would feel to be the first famous musician from Withernsea.

There was no real scene for original music in the town but you could head out any night of the week and catch tribute acts down at the Golden Sands' cabaret suite or the Spread Eagle pub. Cover bands. Pianists. Male/female vocal duos with names like 1970s fragrances. Clandestine. Sophistication. Destiny. A three-piece beat combo called The Johnny Allan Set, who'd been marked for success in the 1960s but never encountered it, would regularly play sets of popular hits at the Victoria Tavern, perched on a small stage in front of a backdrop of shimmering gold tinsel strands. Whenever I listened to music, it was on this stage that I imagined myself playing it, my audience consisting of the people whose approval I wanted. Girls I had crushes on, people who had wronged me. I framed being a successful musician as a multi-purpose tool that would fix all of my problems and elevate me into becoming the kind of person I could respect.

## Track 7

While we waited for someone to respond to the 'Drummer Wanted' sign that I'd put up on the notice board of the newsagents, Alex and I ran reconnaissance missions on what we called 'the competition'. We'd catch bands at Rock Explosion in Bridlington or at Teddy's Nightclub in Withernsea. Here we would measure up other musicians, taking it in turns to periodically holler over the music and into each other's ears. 'WE'RE BETTER THAN THEM!'

As the months passed and our hair grew longer and greasier we made a spectator sport out of this kind of judgement. An East Yorkshire Beavis and Butthead, we issued percussive snorts while we tore apart other bands. Listened only for the flaws. We poured scorn on musicians who played their guitars too high up on their chests or who stood on stage with their legs splayed as if the ground was opening up between their feet. We spotted posers, terrible lyrics, fakes. The more I pointed out the failings of others, the better I felt about my own. There was a lurking sense that I wasn't dedicating myself enough to the hard work involved in being a musician. A discomfort around the fact that I spent more time miming to records than practicing and daydreamed about being gifted the talent to play rather than earning it by learning my scales each day. Still, there was an arrogance that emerged from that insecurity and I wrote a musical manifesto that fitted around my technical limitations, setting goals that allowed for mistakes and failures.

1. Be experimental.
2. Remember that music is Art.
3. There are no wrong notes.

I wrote these words on scraps of paper and pinned them on each wall of my bedroom alongside the few remaining Steven Tylers, reminding myself that I was an artist with a mission. Then I'd stay up late into the night, pounding away at the bass strings, my fingers frustrated by walking basslines and arpeggios.

'You need to stop the fucking writing,' Robert told me one morning, when I came downstairs for breakfast. He was buttering toast, moodily pressing a knife into it. There was a harsh scrape of metal on glaze as it forcibly pierced the toast and connected with the plate. I steeled myself, long wary of an angry Robert with a knife but feeling bold, ready to defend my creative process and explain that he didn't understand my music. But he blindsided me. 'All I hear all night is that fucking typewriter. I promise you now, if you don't give it a rest, I'll come in there and smash it to fucking pieces.'

Robert was staying in the room beneath mine at the time, and he could hear everything I did in there. My singing, the thuds of my dancing, everything, and he had mistaken my practice, the clack of my fingers on unamplified bass strings, for the sound of a dedicated writer tapping out words on the keys. I tried to explain myself to him, but he cut me off.

'I don't care what you *think* it sounds like,' he said. 'It sounds like you're fucking typing. No one wants to hear that.'

After that I switched things up and began dedicating my daylight hours to practicing and my nights to drafting my interview responses and exhaustive lists of career goals, written on the stacks of A4 copier paper that I stole out of the printer at college. While I hadn't dropped out, I coasted through my classes, doing the bare minimum to get by while I redirected my energy into changing the way that music was understood.

'You should be a writer,' my art tutor Harry told me, assessing the sculpture I'd made for my end of term project. 'Because you are very good at making up bullshit.'

My piece consisted of a mangled knot of 5mm steel cable, strung with dozens of parallel cotton threads. It looked like a harp that'd been dragged out of a car wreck, but because Harry had spent the preceding year teaching me how to paint red and explain that it was blue, I'd defended my art as a minimalist commentary on commercialism.

'If anyone else had made this I'd agree it was minimalist,' he replied. 'But because you made it, I know it's laziness.'

But I wasn't lazy, I was working hard. Just not on the right things. I was expanding the manifesto, composing songs and thinking up t-shirt slogans. In essence, I was writing, although I had no idea of that because I had no frame of reference for what being a writer entailed. No more idea of how to write a book than I had about how to assemble a toaster. I could buy magazines featuring cool musicians talking about their origins and how they got their break, but if there was a magazine making writers look exciting to young people, I didn't know about it. There was nowhere I could find a pull-out poster of Kurt Vonnegut looking fuckable. No one I knew was wearing a t-shirt with Joan Didion on the front. I couldn't switch on my TV and see footage of PG Wodehouse, shirtless and dripping with sweat under coloured lights, a crowd swooning before him as he read them extracts from *The Code of the Woosters*.

I was drawn to music in part because it could make you successful if you looked and felt like a weirdo. That this applied to writers even more didn't occur to me at all. That they were the freaks without the garnish and that becoming one would provide me with exactly what I wanted; to be both seen and hidden. But if I thought of writers at all back then, it was dismissively. As sepia-toned author photos on dust jackets, where they showed themselves to be lumpy, hairy creatures. Myopic. Soft. They didn't look like rock 'n' roll, they looked like folk music and that's not how I saw myself. A writer was nothing I wanted to be. I was Art Rock.

## *Track 8*

While I'd been busy scribbling our legend, Alex was operating in reality, conscientiously practicing his guitar and finishing his college projects. He was preparing himself for the future in the way I should have been and this started to peel us away from one another. When it came time to apply for universities he got snapped up by his first-choice Graphic Design degree in Salford, using the 'Cock in Pocket' t-shirt in his design portfolio. I had been hoping to stay close to him and stick to an area of study that left plenty of room for coasting, so that we could still concentrate on our music. But when I sat down with Harry to discuss my university options and told him that I was planning on applying to study Fine Art at Manchester, he insisted that I manage my expectations.

'Don't even bother,' he told me. 'They won't accept you. Apply for Barnsley. You'll get in. They'll take anyone.'

I took Harry's advice and went for an interview, mumbling my way through the panel's questions, laying claim to a love of Joseph Beuys and Ron Arad rather than dEUS or Doo Rag. They flicked through the portfolio of sketches that I'd hurriedly pulled together the previous day and accepted me before I'd even left the room. Our separate paths defined, Alex and I broke away from each other and my tether came loose.

A few months into our first year of study I went to visit Alex in Salford and found that we no longer looked alike. He had started a new band and grown leaner and more angular, favouring tight black clothing that followed the slender, clean lines of his body. He'd cut his hair and dyed it to match his new jeans. A steady diet of Lucky Strikes cigarettes had gifted him with a set of cheekbones so sharp they could plane timber. Meanwhile, I had grown hairier, lumpier, more myopic. In place of smoking, I had taken up eating. Rather than dedicating myself to becoming a songwriter I'd been coming up with short, nonsense stories inspired by Vic Reeves and Spike Milligan, showing them to no one out of concern that I might be told they were terrible. Or worse, that I'd be told they were good, and that I should become a writer rather than a musician.

Back in Barnsley, I joined a band fronted by my housemate Bozz, a twenty-five-stone Iggy Pop wannabe, who had written a catalogue of songs that sounded like '60s garage hits and made me feel nothing at all. We ground our way through gigs and rehearsals, where I tried to concentrate on playing while avoiding Bozz, who howled into the mic and hurled his enormous frame around the stage in thrashing circles, aping the dying rotations of a spinning top. During recording sessions though, he became fastidious and perfectionist. Demanding a level of excellence that was not in my nature.

'That was good,' Bozz would say through my headphones 'but can you play it again? And this time give it a little more … justice.'

I had no idea what that meant, but I knew that it sounded nothing like anything Alex would have ever asked of me, or me of him. I knew that the sound my new band was making was technically good, but I missed the chaos of what Alex and I had. The thrill that every time we played together anything could go wrong and did.

Back in the bedroom of my student house, I'd pose with my bass in front of the full-length mirror on my door, trying to find a way to stand that didn't make my legs look too short or my arms too spindly. But it was clear that my image was not enhanced by a guitar. Place one in my hand and I looked like I was holding it for someone else. As if I was waiting for Alex to take it from my hands with a grateful nod and step out into the spotlight. As time passed and the truth of this became inescapable, these were the things that hurt. The letting go. But of Alex really, rather than the music. When it was the two of us making noise, it filled up both the room and the empty places inside me. Separated from him, music felt like toil. Playacting. The opposite was true for Alex, who had begun to look unbalanced without a guitar, like he was missing a fifth limb. When I'd go to see him play with his new band, I noticed that he'd developed a way of leaning back and wrestling complex sequences of notes from his instrument in a way that didn't look like effort. But it had been. Effort and sacrifice.

Alex would drop out of university during his second year and commit to music completely, giving it precedence over everything. Relationships, jobs, friendships. He was all-in and persistent, his every thought and action dedicated to his music. When I was done with university and exhausted by Withernsea, I moved into the spare room of Alex's flat in Salford and got a job running a high street photo lab. I'd return home from twelve-hour shifts, exhausted and stained with chemical effluent, to see him lugging amps and guitars into waiting vehicles, heading off to rehearsals or pub gigs in nowhere towns. I was jealous of the life he was leading, but really, I pined for him and it was painful to see him not needing me, heading off into a world we should have been entering together. Instead, I was spending my days crouched over strips of negatives and printing holiday photos, watching the highlights of other people's lives flutter by.

In the way things often do when you knock on every door, success eventually came for Alex. He joined a number of bands and toured Europe and Asia. You can buy albums and a DVD with his name on them. He got a guitar endorsement deal and his own Wikipedia page. Meanwhile, though I'd done nothing much of note, I realised I'd succeeded in failing often enough to have something worth writing about. So, I stopped writing nonsense fiction stories and started writing nonsense true ones instead. A few of these got published and I began performing them at spoken word nights in bars and small venues across Manchester, stepping up to mics with a notebook in my hand to tremble under the spotlight, finally daring to reach out for the centre of the stage. Alex and I would watch one another perform, hugging and praising each other's efforts afterwards.

'Fucking ace!' I'd say.

'Fucking ace!' he'd say.

## Track 9

When we catch concerts together these days Alex and I don't critique or judge. We stand at the back and take it all in. Alex bobbing his head, me making notes in mine, tapping my foot to an insistent internal rhythm that has stopped sounding like music, and now only sounds like typing. The last show we attended though, was different. We'd gone to see The Darkness, a band that always brought the two of us joy, but something was bothering Alex. We were in a large venue; I'd watched him perform there just a few years earlier, but his life had changed a lot since then. He'd slowed down. Settled in with his partner and their kids and started working for a company that made mobile crematoriums. Touring and recording had gradually become his infrequent side hustle.

After the encore, when the house lights came on and the crowd began to file out of the venue, Alex held back and let the room empty around him, looking toward the stage. He watched as the road crew dismantled the gear, the floor around him empty, except for me and a thousand abandoned plastic pint glasses. I got the feeling that he was working through something, so I gave him a bit of distance. He stayed like this for a few minutes, staring, before finally letting out a heavy sigh and turning to me.

'Come on,' he said, patting me on the shoulder. 'Let's go.'

When we got outside into the chill night, I pulled my coat around me and chanced a question.

'Do you miss it?' I asked him.

'All the time,' he said, the words sounding relieved, like a long-suppressed confession. He looked as if he was about to say something else then stopped himself and lit a cigarette instead, so I changed tack and started telling him about the book I was working on.

'I'm writing a bit about us,' I told him. 'And our band.'

'Have you made us sound cool?' he asked, then took a deep drag on his cigarette. Exhaled a long, elegant plume. His skin was lined now, but the cheekbones were still the same.

'I've made *you* sound cool.'

'You were cool too.'

'Was I?' I said, surprised that he saw me that way.

He was quiet for a few seconds, looked down, took another drag of his cigarette, exhaled. When he finally turned to answer me, a smile was wriggling across the line of his mouth.

'No!' he said, unable to hold the lie any longer. 'Not at all!'

It was a long time before we both stopped laughing, but while I shouldn't have ruined the moment by keeping track, I noticed that it was me who finished first.

# Blinking Lights and Other Revelations

My elder brother Robert claimed to have seen a UFO. And more than that, that it saw him. It happened during the late '80s. He'd been out in the countryside camping with friends and felt a need to defecate, so wandered over to a nearby cornfield for some privacy. It suited his sense of fun to do it right there in the middle of the field and, as he squatted and lowered his jeans, laughing to himself, a flying saucer shot across the sky from out of nowhere and stopped to hover directly above him.

'It was just like you'd imagine,' he told me, his features alive with the excitement of retelling, throwing his arms wide. 'It was massive and had flashing, multicoloured lights and a big round hole in the bottom with a bright light inside. Like a floodlight but brighter. Like when you look directly at the sun.'

'What did it do next?' I asked, believing every word but always pushing for more of a story. Like it couldn't be enough that some aliens had taken a sudden, intergalactic U-turn to watch my brother taking a dump. But I saw him using the toilet all the time and knew that it was nothing special.

'It started humming and a beam of light came out of the hole and lit me up,' he said. 'It was warm and sort of heavy, like it was pressing against me.'

'And then what happened?'

'It just did that for a while, then the big light switched off and it flew away, really fast. But silently. And then,' he smiled broadly at the memory, 'I had a really, really amazing shit.'

I was about thirteen years old when Robert told me this tale for the first time, six years his junior and probably at my peak of being impressed by him. Everything he did back then seemed like a wild adventure to me. His stories were mostly about fighting, drinking or girls and I'd grown to think of him as a swashbuckling Lothario, tumbling through life in a cloud of fistfight dust and spent condoms. Even the idea of him gracelessly crapping under an extra-terrestrial's gaze seemed somehow magical to me. What made it even more compelling though, was that Robert would stick to this story until the day he died, which was odd as, otherwise, he believed in nothing.

Before staunch atheism was a popular pose, Robert was the only person I knew who dared speak out against God. If evangelical Christians knocked on the door, he'd invite them inside and keep them there, testing their commitment and politeness by forcing them to go through his collection of satanic heavy metal albums or listen to his theories on immaculate conception.

'I think Mary was just a prostitute,' he'd say. 'She got pregnant and when Jesus got old enough to ask her who his dad was, she panicked, told him it was God then it all got a bit out of hand. What do you think?'

'We … erm …'

'Do you think they originally called it Good Friday because killing Jesus was really fun?'

'I …'

'If God is a woman, I bet she has beautiful tits. Do you ever think about that when you're praying?'

This was how he was about all forms of faith and I often wondered how he could be so damning about the beliefs of others yet so convinced by the existence of UFOs.

'Because I've seen one,' he'd say when questioned. 'None of these cunts have met Jesus.'

*

When I outgrew toys and started to become more interesting to him, Robert got into the habit of strolling into my bedroom and milling around, treating it as if it were an annex of his own. I might be sitting on the floor reading or drawing and he'd just walk in and start rifling through my things, picking up anything that caught his eye and, more often than not, slipping it into his pocket. I'd tolerate this, being a little fearful of Robert but also primed to be his rapt and receptive audience. Often, when he tired of stealing from me or asserting his dominance over my territory, he'd throw himself down on my bed, light a cigarette and hit me with the latest edit of his world view. It could be about anything. Music, motorbikes, women, but mostly it was about what he thought was wrong with me.

'You never used to be like this,' he said once, remembering the early years I'd spent terrorising our neighbours and brawling with the other kids on the estate. He'd hoped that I'd become like him and was disappointed when I took a hard left and became his shy, sensitive opposite. 'And you'll never get a girlfriend if you spend all your time in here, reading.' He issued this last word with difficulty, as if the act of saying it made him want to reach for a glass of water to take the taste away.

'I don't just read,' I protested, weakly. 'I draw and …'

'Wank?' he said, gesturing frantically at his waist then raising his hand as if releasing a dove into the sky. I blushed. 'Fucking knew it,' he said, laughing with force. 'You'll never get a girlfriend if you spend all your time doing that either.'

He'd particularly picked up on the fact that I was trusting and gullible, intuiting that it would only take a kindly smile and the promise of free buffet access for me to be lured into a religion. So, he made sure to chip away at any beliefs I might have that he thought of as screwy or spiritual, aware that out in the world I reflected on him. It wouldn't have done for him to be seen in public with a little brother who might suddenly begin speaking in tongues or dropping to his knees in the presence of visions.

One evening, not long after he'd first told me about his UFO encounter, he ambled into my room to find me sitting cross-legged in front of my portable TV, watching Arthur C Clarke's *World of Strange Powers*, a series about the paranormal and the unexplained. The show covered subjects like ghost sightings, poltergeists, stigmata and Uri Geller's ability to stare through the TV and mangle our cutlery drawer. The sorts of phenomena that are now explained away by science or peddled by modern day snake oil salesmen. But Robert was having none of it. Or almost none of it.

'There's no God, no ghosts, no heaven, no afterlife, no angels. It's all bollocks. But aliens …' he said, pausing to take a deep drag on his cigarette and hiss the smoke through his nose. 'Aliens are fucking real, man.'

\*

I thought of Robert's belief often when I first moved to Withernsea and found myself becoming increasingly hopeful of a visit from an alien. It wouldn't have been my first choice. I'd have much preferred a girlfriend or someone to discuss Soundgarden with, but arriving in town I was lonely and desperate to be noticed, so wasn't in a position to be picky. I was aware that there was nothing spectacular about me, nothing really worth causing a fuss about, but my hope was that, while a human would pick up on this straight away, an alien wouldn't catch on so quickly. That they'd see me all alone, bobbing around in the sea or wandering the cliffs and find me intriguing enough to abduct.

Occasionally I would hear stories about UFO sightings further up the coast and bristle with the excitement of possibilities, wondering if one might make its way down to Withernsea and take an interest in me. All kinds of objects had been spotted across the region. Glowing orbs. Cigar-shaped craft. Classic flying saucers that hovered over homes and worried pets into fits of panic. In Whitby, sentient balls of light were said to be luring people along the cliffs towards potential doom. In 1970, at Flamborough Head, just at the northern tip of Holderness, Captain William Schaffner set off from RAF Lincoln in a BAC Lightning jet and crashed into the sea – allegedly in pursuit of a UFO. While his plane was recovered, relatively intact, his body was missing and never seen again, presumed abducted. But most of the sightings seemed to take place from the '90s onwards, following the success of *The X-Files*, when it wasn't unusual to open up a copy of the local paper and read that a UFO had been spotted darting around in cloud cover over Bridlington.

This kind of information was a delight to me back then. Even in a worst-case scenario, should aliens decide to beam me up, vivisect me then fly-tip my ravaged corpse on the crazy golf course next to the promenade, there was still an upside. After all, no one is remembered quite like the disembowelled teenage victim of alien experimentation. You can't buy that kind of attention. If I'd drowned in the sea or fallen from a cliff and broken my neck, my family would have just filed it as typically clumsy behaviour on my part. But there's nothing typical about an autopsy report that reads 'Cause of death: Close encounter.'

If some people in Holderness are to be believed, this kind of contact is not beyond the realms of possibility today. In fact, very little is. The idea that aliens and paranormal entities are treating the Yorkshire coast like a playground is a belief held by many, not least Paul Sinclair, a paranormal researcher from Bridlington. I'd learned about his work when I stumbled across an article in the *Daily Express* about the Holderness town of Wilsthorpe, where, in 2009, an elderly couple claimed to have seen dozens of fifteen-foot boomerang-shaped spaceships hovering outside their seafront flat. Paul was cited as the local authority on the subject, so I looked into his work and learned that he'd been studying the area for twenty years, producing several books and a number of short films about it. He claims that all kinds of wild activity can be found there, in what he refers to as 'areas of high strangeness'. In some ways, his work is no different from my own. We're both fascinated by the region and are studying it carefully, but while I'm interested in people and places, Paul is interested in the intangible. He talks of UFOs, stalking beasts and 'intelligent light forms' that thread their way along the cliffs or descend into the sea to lurk beneath the surface, causing the water around them to bubble like a simmering pot.

Flamborough has been referred to as 'the Bermuda Triangle of the UK' while the *Express* branded Wilsthorpe 'the British Roswell.' It's understandable then that living in this area of the country might have piqued Paul's interest in the paranormal. Still, there's an image you'd build in your head of a UFO hunter and it's not Paul. There's nothing swivel-eyed or crazed about him. He's a stocky, middle-aged man who comes across as the kind of person you'd expect to offer you a reasonable quote to fit some decking, which is exactly the sort of work he was doing before his life transitioned into full-time paranormal investigations.

When I learned that he was looking into a series of mysterious livestock mutilations at Bempton cliffs, just to the north of Flamborough, I emailed him to arrange an interview. I'd read a report about these attacks in the *Hull Daily Mail*, where another paranormal investigator named Mark Vernon was quoted, claiming that something, presumed to not be of this earth, was skinning and disembowelling livestock and marine life around the cliffs near the RSPB nature reserve. It's an area better known for its high concentration of puffins than its unexplained butchery and I wanted to know more about it. But I was also keen to talk to Paul and get a handle on how he became so bewitched by the paranormal that it came to define his place in the world.

'Yes, we can talk,' he wrote back, but when I explained that I was also interested in the work both he and Mark Vernon were doing in Bempton, he became brisk and suspicious.

'Do not link me with the man in the *Hull Daily Mail*,' he replied. 'Regardless of what anyone thinks about unexplained phenomena, I do lots of genuine research. Everything he was talking about was from my work.'

Paul believed that Mark had not only taken credit for his efforts but had gone one step further and found the gall to pose in the press as an expert in the field of werewolf studies.

'People like that,' Paul added, 'do not help anyone.'

This reaction was my first indication that, just as with any belief system, there are schisms and matters of status in the paranormal community. While I waited for Paul to get back to me, I did some research of my own and would quickly learn that the act of laying claim to the work of other investigators is a systemic and rife problem in paranormal society, leading to factions, fallings out, excommunication and feuds. The value placed on such evidence seemed strange when I looked into it and discovered that it wasn't really evidence at all. Or rather, it was evidence, but of the power of belief rather than the existence of supernatural entities. I watched dozens of videos of paranormal enthusiasts narrating blurry, shakily captured footage of pin prick-sized specks of light drifting through the Yorkshire skies, or whispering in excitement at pairs of glowing eyes staring out at them through moonlit scrubland. I listened to hours of broadcasts from paranormal radio stations presented by ufologists and bigfoot hunters, trawled local newspaper archives and looked into the records of mysterious sightings reported to the Ministry of Defence's now-defunct UFO Desk, which members of the public could contact in order to register their experiences of extra-terrestrial lifeforms.

My friend Zoe is scathing about these sorts of things, rolling her eyes and groaning lightly whenever I'd mention that this was what I considered to be part of the 'research' for my book. While I will happily play along with anyone who tells me they've seen a lozenge-shaped spaceship crash land in their garden and ask 'Ooh, what colour was it?', Zoe has no tolerance for this. When I read her some of the UFO Desk reports, her responses to each demonstrated the no bullshit reflexes of a woman who was always inclined to favour Occam's razor.

'July 29th,' I said. 'West Yorkshire: One object, shaped like a cottage loaf. It had a mass of red lights. Sounded like a helicopter.'

'It was a helicopter,' she said, flatly.

'Okay, June 11th, no location given: A man/alien walked

in and laid on the witnesses quilt then whooshed through the window.'

'They were dreaming.'

'Alright, how about March 11th, Bridlington east coast: The object was like an orange and about the same size.'

'Oh, for fuck's sake,' she said, throwing her hands in the air. 'They just saw an orange.'

The most compelling part of my research though, came when I discovered *The Bempton Phenomenon*, a documentary Paul had made with Chris Turner, a paranormal and cryptid investigator from Bolton, covering their investigations into the Bempton mutilations. Cryptids are creatures that are believed to exist despite the lack of supporting evidence. Werewolves, yetis, lake monsters, beasts that for some people remain in the pages of storybooks and, for others, have somehow tumbled from them and set about creating mayhem in our world. It was suspected that the mutilations could be down to one or more cryptids, so Paul and Chris combined forces and set out to find evidence of this.

The film includes a sit-down conversation between Paul and Chris as they discuss their work together and the activity on the cliffs. Paul quickly gets into graphic detail of the injuries sustained by the animals. Sheep with stripped facial skin. Earless, disembowelled deer. Porpoises on the beach with gory puncture wounds. Headless and peeled badgers.

'Who skins a badger,' Paul asks, 'so it looks like it's got a little pair of fur trousers on?'

He questions this in seriousness and bafflement, without realising he'd made the brutal death of an animal sound weirdly adorable, its attacker apparently taking time out from decapitation to enjoy a spot of light tailoring. And while it's not rhetorical exactly, Paul's question is one that Chris leaves unanswered. Because really, what do you say to that?

In one scene Chris interviews a poacher, his image blurred to protect his identity, who tells of encountering a strange and alarming beast on farmland near Bempton Cliffs. The man explained how he was startled by a creature that leapt from the bushes and looked like a baboon, though it was the size of a small horse. Hearing this, Chris nods sagely, rather than doing something reasonable, like rolling his eyes or breaking the fourth wall by turning to the camera and mouthing the words 'What the fuck?'. But my teenage daughter Effie had this covered, having overhead what I'd been watching and finding herself unable to let it slide.

'Sorry,' she said, frowning, her cynical tone one that was sorely missing from the film. 'A man thinks he saw a horse-sized baboon near a puffin sanctuary? Is he drunk?'

'Probably,' I said. 'Some people think it's a werewolf.'

'Why does no one think the puffins did it?'

'I don't think that's plausible.'

'Well, it's more plausible than a werewolf,' she said, placing her AirPods into her ears and cranking up the volume on her phone to drown out the documentary. 'I mean, at least puffins are real.'

This is the kind of logic that you can't argue with, yet people still do. The paranormal exists in a bubble of implausibility. Feeds on it, in fact. It's a world of researchers whose work is almost entirely based on groundless, excitable claims that, through sheer volume, reinforcement and repetition, begin to resemble facts. The glue that holds paranormal communities together is the mutual belief that science does not have the language to address the sorts of phenomena they see in the world.

Beliefs like this take hold along the Yorkshire coast, in large part because it's ignored, if it's ever thought of in the first place. Sunk Island for example, just to the south-west of Withernsea, is known for being the least visited town in the UK. You're about as likely to encounter a traveller from Mars there as you are one from the Home Counties, so a mysterious light in the sky not only provides excitement and intrigue, it also makes the believers here feel chosen. Aliens and cryptid creatures have a whole planet to mess with, but they've picked this coastline to hang out. The locals can feel that there is a specialness in their geographic isolation. That the aliens and monsters come here precisely because it's free from the spotlight, where they can abduct its people and mutilate its livestock in relative peace.

There's no doubt that blaming a mutant baboon for the attacks is more exciting than the more logical notion that a dog is responsible and somehow more comforting than the idea that it was the work of a lone maniac with a machete. It certainly is for people like Paul, who refer to the various types of activity in the area as 'paranormal soup' and believe that the unusual occurrences on this coast are all related. That they have to be. It's one thing to claim that the activity exists in the first place, it's quite another to suggest that it's all part of a single, malevolent truth. Once an idea like the Bempton mutilations gets rolling, every mysterious tale gets caught up in it. UFOs, satanic panic, missing people. Individual incidents from history become evidence to support a unifying and cohesive mystery. When you start thinking that way, it must be hard not to view the world as if there's always a soundtrack of droning, sinister music playing in the background. Once that happens, it becomes natural that a dead sheep found at a bird sanctuary would quickly lead to talk of Captain William Schaffner and a government conspiracy to conceal the truth about alien activity in Yorkshire.

In Holderness, it feels like much of this drive to see the unexplained in the explainable also comes from boredom. When I lived in Withernsea, this was something I felt acutely. Once the allure of the arcades had worn off and the delight I felt at the ready availability of gooey, fresh-fried doughnuts had given way to a fear of diabetes, I often felt a sense of tedium so crushing it was as if the town was subject to its own peculiarly intense force of gravity. I'd kill time by listening to my knockoff Walkman and milling around town, watching other people's lives go by. And in the same way that Paul sees evidence of paranormal activity wherever he looks, everywhere I looked I saw boredom. Bored people in the amusement arcades, sitting at the bingo or listlessly heaving the levers on one-armed bandits. Bored people leaning against the wall outside, smoking, drinking and erupting into feral fistfights just for something to do. And when I caught my reflection in shop windows, I only saw a bored person who looked at bored people. Had an alien appeared at that point, brandishing a scalpel and beckoning me into a spacecraft, I'd have followed them without a struggle, pausing only to grumble 'Well, you took your time.'

Belief is the thing that leaks in through theses cracks, this desperation for *something, anything,* to happen. It spots vacuums that need filling and capitalises on them. Often when things aren't going as planned, you're in the best position to give in to a faith and start believing in something beyond your comprehension. Giving into it can not only be thrilling, it can also be liberating. Look to the blinking lights out at sea in a certain state of mind and you will not see the lamps and torches of ships or the wind turbines but the searching lights of alien spacecraft, and with that perception comes the hope of something more, something bigger. Just as floating in the vast expanse of the sea always makes me feel satisfyingly small and vulnerable, I imagine that a commitment to the paranormal brings some people the same thing. That with this reminder that humans are insignificant in the grand scheme of things, comes a sense of relief. A lack of responsibility that is both freeing and exciting. All I know for certain is that when I was feeling lost and looking for reasons and answers, I discovered that any kind of belief would do and that, once it sets in, it has a way of getting out of control.

*

Towards the end of 2016, when my divorce was being finalised, I needed a place to get my bearings and found myself renting a large, double mezzanine flat on the ground floor of a decon-secrated, portioned-up church. Feeling adrift, I would spend a lot of time alone there, planning my next move and hoping that I'd be able to work out exactly what that would be before I had to commit to another six months on a lease I could barely afford.

Churches are weird places to be on your own, especially when they're also the site where you stare glumly at formerly shared crockery or cram-eat yum-yums while watching re-runs of *Peep Show*. But the one I was living in felt the strangest when I was at the dining table, which was positioned exactly where the aisle would have been. I'd sit for breakfast, thinking of all the married couples who had walked arm in arm where I often sat in my underpants, eating Coco Pops and swearing at breakfast radio. And of the hundreds of coffins that would have been carried through that same space. Then there were the mourners. The bodies subsequently buried in what was then my garden. It had once been a building that absorbed the peaks of life's joy and sadness, the walls and ceiling drenched with prayer, song and the strength of belief. It was tough not to think of that, and fret that I wasn't living up to the demands of the place. I didn't believe that the building was haunted so much, but like discovering that you're standing in a murder house or a place where it's almost certain that Mozart once squatted over a chamber pot, the historical significance of a space can alter the way you feel about it. Inevitably, living in the church would pique my interest in the idea of an afterlife and, with time on my hands, I soon fell into watching ghost hunting videos on YouTube.

Just like the Yorkshire UFO evidence, these videos are made by enthusiastic amateurs, who wander black-clad through graveyards or abandoned mills, filming their excursions with cameras that are incapable of adequately functioning in low-light conditions. Every scene is grainy and dark, the footage reduced to a shifting wash of grey, low-resolution shapes. As a viewing experience it feels like watching a black and white TV through a dirty window, which is exactly the kind of thing you'd expect a ghost to do. Once in a while this gloom is interrupted by one of the investigators turning to look directly into the lens. 'Did you hear that?' they whisper fearfully, in response to the sound of their own panicked breathing.

This is a form of pareidolia, the human quirk of finding patterns and forms in things, like faces in pancakes or hidden messages on Judas Priest albums that order you to shoot yourself in the head. In the same way, these ghost hunters hear the sound of a dripping pipe or a rat scurrying across an asbestos roof and translate it into an angry spirit voice, hissing 'Leave this place!'

I was dismissive of this way of thinking until strange things started happening in my flat. They began in small, irritating ways. The electrics would regularly short out, disabling the heating system. The shower regurgitated clumps of unfamiliar hair whenever I used it. The area under the kitchen sink became mysteriously infested with bluebottles. These are the kinds of things you should expect when rashly moving into a rented property, so when they happened to me, I'd complain to my letting agent and try not to think about them. Then my toilet began to issue boiling water, flowing day and night. Lift the seat and a cloud of steam would rise from it, filling the bathroom until it resembled the set of a Bonnie Tyler music video. My bathroom visits would become masterpieces of efficiency, aware that each time I sat down I was subjecting my testicles to the plumbing equivalent of a rice steamer. Then one morning, sitting downstairs for breakfast, I spotted a patch forming on the living room ceiling. I climbed onto a chair and poked at it with my finger. It felt slimy and spongey. Ectoplasmic. I called my letting agent.

'How big is it?' they asked wearily, long used to the sound of my complaining voice.

'About the size of an orange,' I said, looking up at the ceiling.

'We'll send someone over.'

No one arrived to investigate and over the days the patch continued to grow. I called the agent to report that it had expanded to the size of a grapefruit. Then again when it reached the size of a watermelon. When I ran out of fruits to compare it to, I moved on to sporting equipment.

'It's the size of a medicine ball now,' I told them.

'What's a medicine ball?'

'It's like a basketball but bigger.'

I heard an unsuppressed sigh on the end of the line.

'We'll send someone over.'

I got concerned. The patch grew, the ceiling began to bow. The lights cut out and the toilet hissed angrily in the darkness.

'You should leave that place,' my mother told me, when I phoned her up for advice, illuminated by the glow of my laptop screen, where, against my better instincts, I'd been Googling haunted churches. What I'd learned from Robert was that in order to believe in something I needed first-hand evidence, and the evidence I had gathered was that my home was turning against me.

'I suppose you could hire an exorcist,' my mother suggested. 'Can you do a Google for those?'

My online activity would go on to influence the targeted ads that appeared on my Facebook and I soon began to see regular posts on my feed from a group called The Paranormal Academy. They advertised discounted online qualifications in a number of arcane disciplines. Demonology, Cryptozoology and, most intriguing to me, Ghost Hunting and Paranormal Investigation.

'Do it,' my mother said when I told her about the course. 'I'd like a son who's a Ghostbuster.'

My mother is, spiritually speaking, the anti-Robert. She believes in belief. Christianity-shaped, Buddhism-shaped, Hindu-shaped. Show her a Ley line and she'll straddle it, a third eye painted on her forehead and a crystal in each hand. Between her faith in everything and Robert's faith in almost nothing, I try not to voice an opinion either way. But while I'm generally immune to her spiritual influence, her enthusiasm was infectious, and I signed up for the course that day.

While I sat at my laptop studying residual hauntings and learning how to recognise the presence of shadow people in my home, the patch on my ceiling grew to the size of a space hopper before completely giving way, covering my belongings with a grubby mixture of water and plaster. I called my letting agent in hysterics and they finally sent over a builder who, as he stared up into the hole in the ceiling, explained everything. That the electrics in the flat had been fitted by a rogue construction firm who went bankrupt in the middle of the church conversion and left the job unfinished. And how the remaining work had been completed by another company, who had somehow managed to plumb the hot water tank into the cistern.

'And this is a leak from way up on the roof,' he told me, placing another bucket under the still dripping hole. 'It ran all the way down, picking up hundreds of years of crap as it went, then pissed it all onto your carpet.'

At a time when I'd lost my purpose and was looking for something to latch onto, a cursed building had arrived right on cue to fill my world. I felt stupid after I'd heard the rational explanation and that it had taken so little to push me towards a tentative belief in the supernatural. This knowledge of my own suggestibility would later make me reticent about judging the believers of Holderness too harshly, profoundly aware of how easily a person looking for meaning could spot a paper lantern drifting through the night sky and come to find themselves transformed into a committed ufologist. The idea of paranormal belief rising from a lack of purpose became my default way of understanding it, which made Robert's commitment to the idea of alien existence seem somehow singular because, from my perspective, it seemed that he had everything. That there was no space in him for belief to fill. For Robert, the UFOs came before any desire for a greater meaning but when he did need that support, it intrigued me to see how his interest turned toward the stars.

\*

When he and my niece relocated from Suffolk in the mid-'90s and followed the rest of our family to Withernsea it had been an act of necessity. Unlike my move to the town, which I had only seen in positive terms, Robert's northern restart was not a decision he had revelled in, and it seemed to drain away his drive and determination. His move had followed a series of betrayals in his personal life and an ugly custody battle, which had placed his heart into the rare state of being broken. The confident gusto I associated with him before I'd left for Withernsea had been replaced by something else. If forced to name it, I'd call it loss. Of his autonomy, purpose and identity. For a while, until he established himself with a place of his own, he and my niece moved in with us and I'd often find him standing in the garden at night, smoking and looking up at the sky.

'I wonder if they remember me,' he said one evening, when I headed out to join him.

'Who?'

'The aliens,' he said, turning to me, his brow furrowed as if he couldn't believe I'd just asked such a stupid question. I was forgetting his lesson, that there was no one else up in the sky, just the aliens, so who else could he be talking about? What he didn't know was that I'd stopped believing in his story long ago, having learned more of the context around it. Such as the amount of acid he'd been taking back then or when, leafing through his vinyl collection a few years later, I'd seen exactly the same UFO he'd described pictured on the front of an album by Boston. I'd filed his whole story under drug-induced hallucination, reducing it from a scene of deep significance to something tawdry and disappointing. So, it was strange to hear him speaking in this way, with such a commitment to his story, but also with a note of sensitivity and longing. I'd never seen him pine for anything before, because I'd never seen him go without anything he wanted, his existence seemingly defined by immediate gratification. If he wanted a drink, he'd head to the pub. If he wanted sex, he'd find someone willing. If he wanted a fight, he'd start one. He had always been uninterested in consequences or the future and now here he was, softer and more vulnerable, looking upwards for answers. Meanwhile, left to my own devices and having enjoyed a couple of years away from his sphere of influence, I'd begun to form my own opinions about the world and was starting to put a voice to them.

'You don't still believe in that bollocks, do you?' I said, realising my error while the question mark was still on my lips.

Robert lurched towards me, covering the ground between us at alarming speed, baring his teeth in fury. He judo tripped me and slammed me to the ground, knocking the wind out of my lungs.

'What?' he demanded, standing over me and raising a fist. 'Fucking what?'

'Nothing,' I wheezed, shielding myself from him with my arm.

'Fucking right,' he said, flicking the remains of his cigarette down at me before storming back into the house and slamming the door.

I felt sore and humiliated but also oddly comforted that some of my great certainties still existed. That I could still put my faith in Robert to behave a certain way. In shooting him down I'd been aping him, saying the sort of thing I thought he'd have said to anyone else who might be displaying a perceived weakness. I'd expected him to swear at me rather than shocking all of the air out of my body, but it was a confirmation that the Robert I loved was still there. What I didn't consider was that I'd managed to undermine his faith, and at a time when he'd moved to a part of the country where everyone needed something to believe in. And more than that, he believed that he'd lost my reliable and unwavering belief in him. But you don't think of that sort of thing when someone has just thrown you to the ground, you start thinking of revenge instead, and as I lay in the grass, drawing air back into my lungs, I conspired to make him a conciliatory cup of tea then spit in it.

*

By the time I began writing about the Bempton mutilations I'd learned that, regardless of my scepticism about the paranormal, I needed to treat people's belief in it with respect. I'd make sure to express that respect whenever Paul and I communicated, so this made it all the more frustrating when, while we would get so far as agreeing to a phone interview, he abruptly stopped replying to my messages. I told myself that this was because he is a practical and active researcher who took his work seriously, spending hours camping out on the darkness or trudging through wetlands filming the skies. It's likely that he might have been concerned that my only interest in him was to trivialise his efforts. To make fun. After twenty years of literally and figuratively working in the field, he'd likely have encountered that before.

Denied the opportunity to ask him questions, I tried to pick up on his way of thinking by listening to a number of his many interviews on paranormal radio stations, and it was here that I learned of his belief that the most likely cause of the activity in Bempton could be an interdimensional portal. A thinness between parallel universes that allows paranormal entities to slip from their world into ours, play havoc then slip back home, tidying away the evidence of their presence in the process. How he'd reached that conclusion wasn't clear, but his explanation of how it worked was telling, showing a mind that sought to find a logical order in the illogical. Employing a frame of reference that everyone could understand.

'It's like we're on Radio 1,' he told the host, 'and they're on Radio 2.'

I discussed this explanation with Mark Vernon a few days later. Sore about being ignored by Paul, I'd decided to disregard his warnings and contact Mark in an act of *fuck you* defiance. He was friendly and open, happy for the chance to discuss his work with me and dismissive of Paul's lack of understanding.

'It's not an interdimensional portal,' he explained to me. 'It's actually a gateway.'

'What's the difference?' I asked him.

'Interdimensional portals are used by spirits and gateways are used by physical entities. Cryptids couldn't get in through a portal.'

Mark and Paul's conflict didn't surprise me, oddly because of their similarities. Both enjoy the status their notoriety has brought them and they have a similarly gruff, no nonsense way of speaking about the unexplained, which feels like a contradiction in terms but infuses their claims with a strange kind of earthy legitimacy. That said, there is one big difference between the two of them. Mark claims to have been accompanied on his missions to Bempton by his spirit guide and bodyguard, Kara, a 4000-year-old Sumerian demon from another dimension. Mark explained that they met back when he was visiting a haunted house, where he encountered Kara down in the cellar. They struck up a friendship and Mark began visiting the property regularly to sit down there in the bowels of the building, eating crisps and talking to her using a form of telekinesis, which, when you consider the practicalities, is really the best and most polite way to talk to someone while you're eating crisps. The pair of them now regularly go on adventures together, driving demons and angry spirits from haunted locations all over the country. Their work is part pest control business and part odd couple buddy movie.

By the time we spoke, I'd already spent some time on Mark's YouTube channel watching a video of him confronting the spirits at Knottingley Town Hall in West Yorkshire, attempting to coax Kara into appearing on camera. He spoke to her in the soft, informal way one might use to convince a shy child to sing in public.

'Come on, sweetheart,' he said, 'show yourself.' Eventually a pale blob appeared on the side of the screen. It looked to me like a light flare or a spot of dust floating close to the lens, but Mark called out to her in gratitude, recognising this blob as his companion. 'Come on, baby. That's my girl.' As much as I wasn't buying his schtick, his enthusiasm seemed genuine. Just like Paul, he didn't come across as a shyster; he sounded like a true believer. But even for Mark, there were limits.

'I don't believe in God because I've never met him,' he told me. 'And I don't believe in werewolves.'

'So, what do you believe is killing the animals at Bempton?'

'I think it's something to do with UFOs,' he said. 'They're coming through a gateway for some reason. There's nothing in nature that can do what they're doing. It's like the animals have been blown up from the inside. Kara refers to them as *Them*.'

'And these are the entities that are killing sheep? *Them*?'

'Yes.'

'Could a human not be doing it?'

He laughed at this. 'Have you ever tried to catch and kill a sheep?'

'No.'

'Well, there you go then.'

This was paranormal QED and I should have been used to it by that point. I changed tack.

'Why do you think there's a particularly strong belief in this sort of thing along the Yorkshire coast?'

'Well, they say there's something going on in the cliffs. Maybe something living in there. Tunnels. People have seen creatures crawling up the cliff face. All that and the aliens. It's all related.'

'Do you not think there's a chance that the people who live there could just be bored and making these stories up?'

'What would they have to gain from that?' he asked, incredulous.

I took a beat then, aware that I'd talked myself into a cul-de-sac where I might have to admit that I found Mark's story to be exactly the kind of thing that someone would make up because they were bored and wanted attention. That they just liked getting in the newspaper. Whether he noticed this or not, he gave me an out.

'I'm going back to Bempton soon,' he said. 'I'll let you know how we get on. Kara's shown me a location where they're coming through.'

We pledged to speak again once his investigation was complete, and Mark made his goodbyes with an offer to summon Kara in my presence the next time he was in Manchester.

'I like to put my money where my mouth is.'

Our conversation had created more questions than it answered, but it did help prove the existence of something – that 'paranormal soup' does appear to exist, just not in the way Paul Sinclair thinks it does. It's a soup of boredom, altered mental states, faith, drug psychosis, a need for adventure and a drive to believe in something beyond the day-to-day. Most of all though, it feels like it comes from a need to belong, to feel special. For the men and women researching these phenomena, it's about the thrill of the hunt. They're like gamblers, bingo players, one armed bandit addicts, always looking for that high.

\*

To overcome my annoyance at being ignored by Paul, I'd been quietly telling myself that he'd probably been eaten by the beast of Bempton. That his silence might be because his hands and larynx were occupied with the act of being digested in another dimension. If not a comforting explanation exactly, it at least amounted to an Out of Office reply. He would have got back to me, but unfortunately, he was dead. This theory was thrown out of the window when I received a notification from his YouTube channel, informing me that he'd posted a video update on his werewolf investigation. The thrill of the hunt was still very much in effect.

'I never ever thought I'd be discussing things of this nature,' Paul says, before the video cuts to footage of him picking his way by torchlight through the darkness of Bempton Cliffs and detailing his evidence of a new werewolf sighting, submitted to him by an ex-paratrooper who'd been for a few drinks then gone wild camping in the area with a friend. A recording of their conversation plays over eerie images of absolutely nothing happening on the cliffs.

'I thought it looked like a fucking hyena,' the man says at first, in an excitable Liverpudlian lilt. Very quickly, his description begins to evolve. 'It fucking stood up. It stood up on two fucking legs. It was about seven-foot tall, mate.'

'Did it have a long face?' Paul asks.

'It had a long snout, yeah.'

'And the ears, were they stood up at the side of the head?'

'The ears were pointy at the side of the head.'

'Did you see owt on the end of its ... are we calling them hands or claws?'

'I'd say claws, mate.'

It was like listening to a coerced confession, Paul seeming to nudge his preferred responses out of the witness. The man had started off talking about having seen a creature that resembled a wild dog and ended up describing what sounded suspiciously like the werewolf in the movie adaption of *The Prisoner of Azkaban*.

As much as I was annoyed with Paul at this point, I didn't believe that he was doing this cynically or knowingly. What I heard was the sound of a man so compelled by a particular viewpoint that he was trying to bend the world to fit it. Once you latch onto a set of beliefs and surround yourself with people doing likewise, it's easy to see how those beliefs can take root and begin to resemble undeniable, cast-iron facts. Past that point it stops being unlikely that Flamborough Head would have both UFOs and an interdimensional entry point for *Doctor Who* villains. It has UFOs *because* of the interdimensional entry point, and why wouldn't extra-terrestrials come to visit that?

All that Paul's new evidence proved was that I wasn't going to get the answers I wanted from him or from Mark or from countless hours of internet deep dives. The only way to really do it was to find out first-hand. So, armed only with a million-candle torch, a need to be right and a small, maybe, just maybe, thrill that I might be wrong, I put my dog Millie in the car, and we drove to the North Yorkshire coastal town of Filey, where my parents keep a caravan. This was during the summer of 2020, when COVID-19 restrictions meant I could travel, but that there would be fewer holidaymakers around to disturb a werewolf mid-rampage. Stationed at the caravan, I could rise at around one a.m. each morning and set out to the paranormal hotspots I'd learned about, looking for the evidence with my own eyes. I had half a mind that Millie would act as some kind of protection, but she was in a deep sleep when I woke, her old bones too exhausted for adventures, so I journeyed alone to Bempton, Flamborough and Wilsthorpe. Drove from Hunmanby to Flixton to Dane's Dyke, where other werewolf sightings had been reported, scrabbling through woodland and peering across fields of swaying wheat for signs of supernatural life. By day, each of these locations could double for Miss Marple's St Mary Mede, all white-painted stone cottages and well-tended hanging baskets that spewed vivid blooms, but driving through them at night, where there are very few streetlights and miles of pitch-black road, you don't see obstacles until they're upon you. It's easy to see why people could find an eerie significance in this land. Step out of the car and the sensation is amplified. Every sound makes your skin bristle. The howling wind, the rush of the sea, the shriek of the birds and the random barks that could come from terriers or feral beasts who had caught my scent and were racing towards me through the long, violently parted grasses.

On one of these night missions, I parked up at a passing point on the road that leads to the RSPB nature reserve at Bempton Cliffs and stood at my open car door, keeping it between me and whatever might be out there roaming the land. Behind this shield, I waited, and I wanted. More than anything what I wanted was to see the aperture of an interdimensional gateway opening up, and to watch as an ape-wolf with matted fur and shifty red eyes stepped through then jump over the bushes to feast on the spoils of our world. I wanted to see it, film it clearly and have all this be worth something. Maybe to have Robert proved right and gain evidence that this sort of thing wasn't actually bollocks after all. But also because, not so long ago, I'd have welcomed death by any means and getting taken out by an interdimensional werewolf would have been a hell of a way to go. To be torn apart and left for Paul or Mark to discover. With time on my hands and nothing to do but stare and ponder, I found myself thinking of that old Stuart Chase quote about the nature of belief.

'For those who believe, no proof is necessary. For those who don't believe, no proof is possible.'

Still, what better way was there to make a believer out of me than to feel a set of monstrous claws unzipping my chest and emptying my guts onto the ground? But ten minutes of staring out into the unchanging darkness turned to twenty, thirty, an hour, and the giddy fear that I might become the victim of a werewolf or even a homicidal human gave way to a greater one of death by hypothermia or my old friend boredom. So, I got back in the car, turned it around and headed back to the caravan, switching on my heated seats.

Driving back, the warmth of the seat against my back and thighs seemed to combine with my exhaustion and my eyesight began to feel somehow woolly. I'd just opened my window to let some cool air in and stop myself from nodding off at the wheel when I spotted a glow rising in a hazy semi-circle from behind the brow of a hill. I felt a rush of excitement that caused my buttocks to clench as if a tight zip had been yanked up between them. The light was swaying, shifting left and right as it grew in intensity. Washes of white and orange which, despite the rumbling sound of my diesel engine, I felt that I could hear. It seemed to be pulsing. Issuing a kind of bassy throb.

'Fucking hell …' I said out loud, my heart pounding and the blood in my hands seeming to prickle and buzz as they gripped the steering wheel. Because I was driving, I couldn't take a photo. The road I was traveling along was narrow with high, dense bushes on either side, so I couldn't stop anywhere. I would only have my word as evidence, and what good was that? *This is how it happens*, I thought. *This was how I'd become one of those people, someone who'd had an encounter, could provide no evidence of it and would be cursed to spend the rest of their life being thought of as a fantasist and a crank.* Then the source of the light rose over the hill and I finally saw it clearly for what it was, looming out of the darkness like a deep-sea fish. A double decker bus, every light inside it blazing. It rattled towards then past me, the driver wearing headphones and singing along to music only he could hear. I watched it in my rear-view mirror as the blaze of its lights was reduced to the size of an orange before being swallowed up by the darkness.

Had I been bored or stoned or addled by some other mental state, I could have still convinced myself that what I'd seen was a UFO lurching into view, even as the bus had rushed past me. Especially if that was what I'd been looking for and had wanted to see more than anything else. If I was so lost and in need of feeling chosen. I know there were times when I'd felt that need before and would have leapt towards the first saviour that came my way, but out there in the dark, although I was ready for anything, I knew a bus when I saw one.

I'd spent countless hours standing out there on the cliffs or watching the skies, camera at the ready, prepared to be open-minded and channel the gullible and hopeful version of myself, but I ended up seeing nothing except the incredibly ordinary. What's more, I felt hollow. There was no excitement for me, no belief, no chase. I'd made room in myself to be filled by God or monsters or aliens or whatever else might be out there and what I ended up feeling was a crushing emptiness. I was done with it all.

With no space left in me for belief, I finally turned to Occam's razor. I headed back to the caravan, switched on my laptop and Googled 'animal mutilations'. I'd avoided doing this sooner, I think because I wanted there to be more going on here. I didn't want the dull and simple cynics answers, but within half an hour, I had some. Not dull exactly, but very much of this world. I learned that the porpoise injuries were a grim by-product of bass fishing, caused by them getting caught up in fishing nets or mortally wounded when fishermen attempted to cut them free. The sheep mutilations were a result of illegal butchery, killed and carved up in situ by those wishing to sell meat on the black market and knowing that it's easier to transport a leg of mutton than a whole sheep. Captain William Schaffner, it turns out, died simply because he flew too low and crashed into the sea. His son, Michael, backs this conclusion and is angry at anyone who suggests otherwise.

'I am completely satisfied that my father died because of a chain of unfortunate events, none of which had anything to do with someone's subjective need to believe in UFO's.'

As for the horse-sized baboon, well that was just the drink talking.

I closed my laptop, woke Millie and the two of us took the short walk from the caravan and over to Filey cliffs, where I took a seat on one of the benches that overlooked the beach. From there I could watch as the sun came up and slowly illuminated the cliffs over at Bempton and Flamborough, Millie snuffling at the grasses, catching scents. I saw a lot of things while sitting there. Bats, gulls, fishing boats and, high above them all, the fierce pin-prick light of Venus, but I didn't see any mysterious orbs tracing the cliff edge or alien figures crawling up the chalk face. No silhouetted werewolves nipping back through an interdimensional gateway. I knew that I could sit out there for a decade and the closest I would get to evidence of the paranormal would still come from Robert, the sincerity in his eyes as he told me of his UFO encounter more tangible than anything I'd discovered while researching the Bempton mystery.

It was hard then to stop myself from considering the months before he died, when his life was slipping off the rails again. Of how he'd taken to sneaking out of his house at night while his wife and children were asleep and taking long walks along the coastline, trying to work out if there was a way forward for him. I thought of him making this journey, reaching the rural land on the edge of town and an idea occurring to him, out there in the dark. I pictured him climbing over a fence, heading out to the middle of a field and looking up to the stars. Searching the skies for a darting spot of light, his body braced and ready, hopeful that the ship would come back for him.

# Consider the Birds

If you stand on the beach at Withernsea on a clear day you can see the Netherlands. If you stand there on a gloomy one, you will get the sense that there is nothing worth seeing nor will there ever be again. But between the Netherlands and depression, you will see wind farms. There are thirty-five towering, white turbines at Westermost Rough. Another seventy-three just east of Spurn Point, at Humber Gateway. There are nine more inland between the small towns of Roos and Burton Pidsea. And soon there will be Hornsea Project One, the world's largest wind farm, covering an area the size of fifty-eight football pitches.

From a distance the turbines look dainty and fragile, like windmills made from glue and paper straws, an infants' school craft project laid out to dry. But stand beneath one and you will see that it resembles the detached leg of a giant robot, yanked from its socket and left behind when the rest of it shot off into space. And this is one reason why, when they first began to appear along the Holderness coast, the turbines had a way of dividing opinion.

*

There are very few growth industries in this part of the country, but the North Sea wind has always been to Holderness what oil is to Texas. It's what carves gullies into the features of the sea-facing locals and slams the waves into the clay cliffs, whittling them back to the chalk base. In some ways, these farms are evidence of the region's ability to make lemons into lemonade; if you can't farm the land because the wind has destroyed it, then you might as well farm the wind. But when the planning applications were originally submitted in the late '90s, the people of Holderness took against wind turbines with a fervour you'd expect them to reserve for an advancing enemy army. They formed protest groups, launched a campaign and – in a field on the outskirts of Withernsea – organised an anti-wind farm concert.

I wasn't on board with this crusade. Wind turbines may be imposing but even back then I thought they were a good idea. At the very least they seemed like a decent alternative to mining the earth until it became as hollow as a value-brand easter egg. What's more, they're pretty much as beautiful as it's possible for a giant metal structure to be. Pale, streamlined and elegant, if they were the size of a desk fan they'd be slapped with an exorbitant price label and presented in John Lewis alongside zesty-coloured KitchenAid mixers and £30 bars of bergamot soap. This made the anger they caused even more fascinating to me and, figuring that I could combine the concert with a visit to see my family, I jumped in my car and drove over to Withernsea to see what the fuss was all about. At worst, I told myself, it would be a bad concert in a field and that could at least be funny. But as the evening progressed, I would begin to feel as if I was in a coma dream, having fallen asleep at the wheel on the outskirts of town.

Driving to Withernsea on the evening of the concert, my headlights picked out a lot of small details. There were the things I expected to see, like the flash of a cat's eyes or the profile of a sudden, darting fox. Then there were the things that I didn't expect, such as the legion of twenty-foot wicker men guarding the fields on either side of the road as I got closer to the concert site.

The roads into Withernsea are as winding and treacherous as vipers and even by day I drive along them with the same level of caution I would apply to removing a block from the base of a teetering Jenga tower. Heading down the A1033 you're as likely to pass a crashed hatchback resting like an upturned bug in the roadside brambles as you are a gambolling horse or a common blackbird. Still, at their best the roads into the town are pleasing and picturesque, running through fields of wheat and rapeseed so yellow you could believe they're attempting to outdo the sun. On this night though, they were drenched in a deep, inky darkness that I was particularly struck by as a consequence of having moved to Manchester, where the night sky never gets any darker than the sooty orange you'd associate with the glow from a house fire. Adding to the threat of the roads and appearing suddenly out of that dense night, these giants stood. Towering figures constructed from stacked hay bales, each of them painted with ghastly, enraged faces.

It's a misnomer to call them wicker men really. They weren't made of wicker for a start, and you'd have struggled to trap a house cat in one, let alone a curious out-of-town police officer, but it stands up as a neat visual shortcut. Had a wild-haired Christopher Lee been standing beside them, brandishing a flaming torch, he certainly wouldn't have looked out of place. These giants had a purpose beyond the pagan though, and as my full beams illuminated them, I saw that each bore a slogan spray-painted in slashing capitals.

'NO TO WIND FARMS!'
'WIND FARMS OUT!'

When I parked up outside the concert site and stepped out of the car, I heard more of the same – a call and response chant from somewhere in the darkness of the fields. A mob of angry voices.

'WHAT DO WE WANT?'
'NO WIND FARMS!'
'WHEN DO WE WANT IT?'
'NOW!'

The way these words fell was jarring, like a passage in German scrambled into English by Google Translate. But if there was ever a good time to judge the grammar of passion, it wasn't right then, in the middle of a protest. The shouts made me trepidatious, but as I entered the site I was surprised to discover that the atmosphere was upbeat. The cause had clearly been retooled as an excuse for a good time and a decent-sized crowd was eagerly awaiting the performance of a local cover band, who were setting up on the flatbed truck that doubled as a stage. The chanting, it seemed, was just something unifying to occupy a few members of the audience while the bass player tuned up, and I felt pretty relaxed as I wandered through the site, looking for someone I recognised. I quickly spotted one of the town's two David Bowie impersonators, dressed in his Modern Love-era attire, and just beyond him, my mother, who was standing beside a slew of entries for a protest poster competition that had been pinned up onto a sheet of hardboard. A frieze of technicolour scribbles and bubble writing. I waved as I headed over to her and she met me halfway, greeting me with a tight, enthusiastic hug.

'Do you want to see some flying pigs?' she asked as she released me.

'Have you been drinking?'

'Yes,' she replied. 'But that doesn't change my question.'

This made more sense when she led me over to her competition entry, which depicted a drove of winged pigs being chopped into pieces by a huge spinning turbine. They fell from the skies, squealing 'SAVE US!', while rashers of bacon fluttered from their lacerated rumps like air-dropped leaflets.

'What the hell is that?' I said.

'The judge called it third prize,' she said proudly. 'Third prize is still winning.'

She was repeating something I'd often said to her during childhood, my competitive career largely distinguished by a selection of medals for taking part.

'So, which one got first prize?'

She pointed bitterly to a poster in the centre of the board. I don't remember much about it, except that, like all of the other entries, it was drawn by a child and centred on saving birds. Specifically, gulls.

'The turbines are killing them,' my mother told me, as I paused in front of an image of a herring gull looking mournfully at a turbine, tears cascading from its eyes. 'They don't know how to avoid the blades and just fly straight into them.'

'Why?' I said. 'Can't they just move a little bit to the left and fly around them?'

'I don't know, but it's true. Ask anyone.'

As the evening progressed, I did just that, asking protesters their thoughts and hearing this argument over and over. The wellbeing of the gulls seemed to be on everybody's mind.

'They can't fly fast enough to get through the blades, so they get sliced in half,' a woman told me later, shouting over the noise of the band, now fully tuned-up and grinding out blues standards. Her friend chipped in and cranked this idea up to eleven.

'You might as well put them in a blender,' she said, yelling into my ear. I pictured this image and winced, feathers and guts whipping around, the noise of a stuttering blade working its way through a bony obstruction. While the band loudly wrestled with their version of 'The Green Manalishi', the only sound I could think of was the one in my head, of turbine on bird. 'It's actually illegal to kill seagulls,' the woman added. 'So, technically it's murder.'

Mass murder wasn't the only protest argument being used. I was told that turbines were expensive and inefficient. That every time the blade spun it issued a concussive sonic boom. And also, that they just ruined the view and people didn't want them around. That the main thrust of this campaign was to protect gulls confused me though, as I had long considered them to be monsters. It was especially tricky to get my head around as this notion, like many of my enduring beliefs, came from my mother.

*

When I was young, she would often talk about the heatwave during the summer of '76, the year I was born. She'd explain how it was so hot that it disrupted the whole country. Crops failed. Forest fires broke out. Reservoirs dried up and sheets of sunburned skin flaked off people's shoulders like old, peeling paintwork. But mostly what she talked about was the gulls.

'They were so thirsty they were plucking the eyes out of lambs,' she'd tell me, as if there was no other option. No other source of fluid left for them but the juice that could be squeezed from an innocent young eyeball. She always said this with a note of horror, as if all nature needed was the right set of circumstances to turn against us all. 'When they run out of lamb's eyes,' she wanted to say. 'They'll come for ours.'

Hearing her tell this story for the first time I was immediately resistant to it. The inference that I was not as safe from nature as I might like to think undermined some of my greatest certainties. Growing up, my family nickname had been St Francis and I was known for my affinity with nature. I would capitalise on any opportunity to follow a squirrel up a tree or conduct a conversation with a passing frog. If I wasn't doing that I could be found in front of the TV, blanketed by our family pets and watching nature documentaries, dreaming of all the different creatures I could befriend while percolating a growing ambition to one day cuddle a lion.

As a child in rural Suffolk I'd learned to think of my surroundings as a comfort and a solace. I could step out of my house and within a few minutes disappear into what amounted to a painting by Constable. Hours were spent waddling along the banks of Stour Brook in search of sticklebacks and frogspawn, the only sound that accompanied me being the rustle and snap of unseen wildlife wriggling through my surroundings. I'd travel for miles beneath skies so speckled with birdlife they resembled a starlit night in negative. To look up and be fearful, to think that all that time I was just one weather event away from a bird swooping down and carrying my juicy young face back to its nest, was an unbearable concept.

So, rather than absorb my mother's story and accept that the world I loved might be capable of turning on me, I looked to my father, who considers the natural world to be something pure and good that must be monitored and cared for, like a beloved, ageing relative. My memories of the warmth in his smile when I'd excitedly announce that I'd identified a nuthatch or a greenfinch in our garden are precious to me, tempering those of him on my school sports day, looking disappointed as he watched me trying to run with dignity. I hoped to find in him the reassurance I needed, but what I found was more troubling evidence of the monstrousness of mother nature.

'Oh, it doesn't make sense to steal their eyes,' he'd said, dismissively. 'They're probably just using the eye socket as the quickest path of entry to the brain.'

Had I been a different type of child I might have said, 'Wow, what the fuck, dad?' but instead I pushed this knowledge deep down and tried not to think about it. This was something I was doing a pretty good job of until my high school art teacher, Mr Clarke, introduced new evidence.

'All she would paint was seagulls,' he told me. 'Over and over. Just … seagulls.'

I must have been around 14 at the time and he'd been standing by my desk, explaining the story of a girl who had taken his class a few years earlier. He stared away into his memories as he spoke.

She'd been on holiday, he'd said. Sitting on the beach with a picnic, when she was set upon by a flock of seagulls. They didn't want her, he was sure. They just wanted her sandwiches. But she'd flapped and yelled. Fought back, wheeling her arms. So, they went for her instead, until all of the sandwiches were gone, and she'd been left with some nasty cuts and a morbid fear of gulls.

'I just let her carry on painting them,' he said, his hand absently stroking the air with an invisible brush. 'I hoped it'd get them out of her system eventually.' He paused. Sighed. 'Didn't work.'

*Don't eat near gulls*, I thought. *Don't fight back. Don't let them see your juicy young eyeballs.*

*

I had spent most of my life being fed the information that gulls, like sharks or tarantulas, inhabited that peculiar area of nature that it was okay to not be sentimental about. Yet there I was, standing in a field full of people who were pulling for them. It was confusing, like being at a cancer benefit where everyone was rooting for stage four lymphoma. Still, the fact that the protest had been so much about the innocence of gulls lingered with me, threatening to overturn a lifetime of belief. Sympathy for their plight was new to me and staying over at my parents' house that night, lying in my old bedroom, my old bed, I found myself thinking about gulls in distress. Gulls falling. Gulls sliced and diced. Gull chicks in nests, starving to death while waiting for parents who would never return because they'd been chopped to pieces by a megastructure.

I woke up early the next morning and slipped out of the house to take a walk along the promenade. This has always been a part of my routine whenever I visit Withernsea, to get up around dawn, clear my head and check out the sea and the progress of the dwindling cliffs. That morning though, it was also to consider the gulls. The air was crisp, and a cutting wind forced me to take refuge in a seafront shelter, where I sat for a while watching sea birds wheeling about in the sky and cawing, trying to think of them without preconceptions. To recalibrate myself. What if I decided to look at them with no baggage, with none of the grisly stories? How would I think of them then? I'd been sitting there for maybe half an hour, mulling this over, when I spotted an old man in a woolly hat and a heavy coat slowly making his way up the promenade towards me. The wind was buffeting him, and his right hand leapt to his head to keep his hat in place, his left held out almost daintily at his side, assisting his balance. When he finally reached the shelter, he lumped down beside me with a heavy sigh.

'Blimey!' he said. 'I thought I was in the sea then.'

We soon got talking, about the weather and such, and after a while fell into a discussion about the windfarm protests and the gulls.

'I ate a gull once,' he told me, looking up at one screaming above us.

'Really?' I said, leaning in, keen to know more. Forgetting that I was there to give gulls a second chance and suddenly only interested in details of a dead one. I wanted to know why he'd done it. How it had tasted. Everything. It had been during World War II, he said, and he'd been desperate for food. The sight of it, all large and proud-breasted, made it too tempting to resist. 'Big bugger, it was. It looked delicious.' But upon shooting it and cutting it open, he was immediately disappointed. There was less meat than he'd expected, gulls being light and mostly bone, conducive with flight but not, apparently, a cultured palate.

'But what did it taste of?' I asked.

'Of what it ate,' he said. 'Rotten fish, rubbish, crap. It was revolting.'

Its insides, he added, were home to a foul, black goo. 'That sounds right,' I said, thinking this was precisely the kind of substance that I'd expect to find inside something with such a proven track record of scurrilous behaviour. Looking up at the gulls then, my sympathies faded and I began to think of them as rotting, airborne piñatas filled with festering, treacle-coloured fluid. Had I pulled out a gun at that moment and shot one from the sky, I'd have half expected it to burst like a water balloon and trigger the gag reflex of everyone within a 100-metre radius. It seemed to me then, that, if the wind farms were as dangerous as I'd been told the night before, the only downside was that it'd become some poor soul's job to sweep up the mounds of fetid, black gull slurry that would inevitably collect around the base of the turbines. A price worth paying.

*

As is often the way when small town interests come up against big business, the anti-windfarm campaign ultimately came to nothing and turbines began to appear across Holderness like a remarkably successful species of self-seeding tree. First, they were erected sparingly on land. Then, as the years ticked by, they appeared out to sea in greater and greater numbers, coming to dominate the horizon. The secret of their success seems, in part, to be down to the energy companies offering annual pots of community funding to the towns closest to the turbines in exchange for the people of those towns shutting the hell up. Once that happened, it wasn't a great leap of visual imagination for people to stop thinking of wind farms as murderous, towering abominations and starting to look at them as money trees. When it later transpired that turbines were actually near the bottom of the list when it came to bird mortality statistics, those with a taste for campaigning moved on and began to focus on raising funding for sea defences or a new pier.

The annual estimate of bird deaths caused by wind farms in the UK is somewhere around 106,000. This looks like a big number until you consider domestic cats, which each year kill fifty-five million birds for sport, and windows, which dispose of roughly twice that number. The exclamation point on this is that the RSPB had a wind turbine fitted to their head office. Not in the way that churches erect crucifixes, more as a gesture on their part to recommend that people calm ... the fuck ... down. When you stop to consider that your parents' conservatory is more capable of avian genocide than a 100-foot spinning blade, you start doubting every belief you've ever had. Unlike a faith, which can really only be lost or found, belief is malleable and if you stop a local on the seafront these days and ask them their opinion of the wind farms, they tend to speak of them with tones of pride.

'We're going to have the biggest wind farm in the world,' they'll say, pointing towards Hornsea and a space that will one day be nothing but giant spinning blades.

But every now and then, I'll encounter someone who feels uneasy about the rise of the turbines.

'I think there's something eerie about them,' Angela told me, from her clifftop chalet at the Golden Sands resort, the view of Westermost Rough as familiar to her as the sight of the rising sun. 'At night,' she said. 'You can just see the lights out there and they look ... alien.'

I understood this suspicion of their extra-terrestrial aesthetic: smooth, white, towering. Giant outsiders disrupting the horizon line, in this land of paranormal rumour, but they have arrived with good intentions. Not issuing a gravel-toned order of 'Take me to your leader' the gentle grind of their blades sounds something closer to 'We have come to save you.'

My mother recognises this and has had a complete turna-round. For her, there is no longer a sense of threat when she looks out at the turbines. Instead, she sees what I see.

'I think they're majestic,' she told me, regarding the view of them from the promenade as we walked along it on a clear day during the summer before the pandemic. 'Really beautiful.'

While I enjoyed the feeling of having been proved right, I struggled with the idea that Withernsea had let its guard down. It seemed to me that, by protesting against the turbines, the people had softened their stance on gulls and had made them-selves vulnerable to threat from above. I hadn't though, instead I'd been building up a dossier.

It started as a joke, as a way of messing with my mother, who had decided that just because turbines weren't what they'd first seemed to be, it didn't mean that gulls were automatically being put back on nature's naughty list.

'I like them,' she said.

'You said they were monsters!'

'Don't be daft, that was the 1970s. Those birds are long dead.'

To her, saying that I was concerned about seagulls from 1976 was like saying I was scared of The Yorkshire Ripper or the increasing popularity of disco. In truth, it's because my mother is as stubborn as I am. She'd been forced to do an about-face on gulls in order to support the campaign against wind farms, and because she'd already capitulated on that I couldn't expect her to easily commit to another reversal of opinion.

'Seagulls are our friends now,' she said, intentionally over-egging her position for comic effect, but I made a thing of it. Wouldn't let it go.

'Name one seagull that's your friend.'

'Christopher,' she said, after a brief pause.

'Christopher the seagull? That's what you're going with?'

'Yes, Christopher the seagull.' Her words were made of concrete and steel, no movement at all. 'I see him all the time. I'll introduce you. You'd like him.'

'I'll look forward to it.'

'Alright then.'

'Alright then.'

So, to spite my mother, I set about proving that 'Christopher' and all of his kind, were bastards. Every time I'd come across a negative seagull story in the paper, a sidebar about a gull stealing a man's hat or attacking a picnicking family, I'd clip it out and send it to her in the post, with a note attached.

'I see Christopher's in the news again. Have a word.'

When she got a smartphone, I started sending her links to videos of gulls caught in the act of committing crimes. I sent her footage of a gull entering someone's house through the window and eating their fish and chip dinner off the kitchen counter.

'Aww, Christopher,' she replied. 'He thinks he's a person.'

'You're not supposed to say aww,' I told her. 'You're supposed to think he's dreadful.'

'Awww.'

I sent her other stories of gulls causing mayhem, noticing that the reports tended to accuse them of displaying negative human traits. One was reported as 'arrogantly' stealing a packet of crisps from a Greggs and upon leaving the store accused of displaying 'no shame'. Another attacked its own reflection in the bumper of a car before being deemed 'dim-witted' and 'vain'. A woman spotted some angry seagulls gathering around a dead animal in the street and 'acting suspiciously.'

'I see Christopher's joined a gang,' I told my mother, when I sent her this last story.

'Everyone needs friends,' she said.

'I thought you were his friend?'

'You need more than one friend. I can't be his everything.'

We kept this up for years and while it was all a bit of a game, I couldn't help noticing over time that the stories I'd come across had started to take a darker turn. Reports came in of gulls swooping down into gardens and mutilating small family pets in full view of screaming families. The headlines were alarmist, and it soon became clear that the press was rebranding gulls as airborne Vikings, determined to pillage the entire circumference of the UK.

During the summer of 2015, the rise in gull misdemeanours was finally highlighted as a national problem and the country began to consider itself at war. Guidance was issued for protecting oneself from attack and the Prime Minister, David Cameron, held a press conference, explaining the dire need to address the issue.

'I think a big conversation needs to happen about this,' he said. 'We do have a problem.'

Watching this was like witnessing an establishing scene from a sequel to Hitchcock's *The Birds*. My fears were being realised and I had confirmation from the highest level that I was now living in a time where I could expect to be swarmed and pecked hollow by black-backed gulls the moment I stepped out of my front door. And that maybe I should start making my daughter wear her bicycle helmet and swimming goggles when she played in the yard.

'We're losing bees and gaining seagulls,' my colleague Denis said when we saw this report on the news. 'We get the birds we deserve'.

This sounded like a corrupted version of the idea from *Peter Pan*: that every time a child denies the existence of fairies a fairy dies. But in Denis's version, every time someone throws a pissy tantrum in Starbucks or gives in to road rage, a bee keels over and a herring gull blinks into existence then fucks up a chihuahua. But what he really meant was that this was society's problem. Just like it's possible to poorly raise a child or a dog, it's possible to influence the natural world around us to a negative effect, and there were consequences of that.

Following the Prime Minister's announcement, it soon became impossible for me to *not* think about gulls, so I went all in and decided to keep track, setting up a Google news alert for stories that featured them, inviting a daily update to flutter into my inbox and trigger me. These stories were not big on environmental science and existed more as a gathering point for lurid detail. Each followed the same rough template: an alarmist headline, a vivid description of a brutal incident, a hyperbolic quote from a concerned local and a photo that allowed you to stare into the open beak of a mad-eyed gull then shudder.

'BRITISH SEAGULLS ARE TURNING CANNIBAL AND EATING EACH OTHER,' screamed *The Sun*.

'SEAGULL TEARS OUT CAT'S TONGUE,' cried the *Daily Mail*.

'SEAGULLS DROP "CAT OR PUPPY PAW" IN CITY CAR PARK IN FRONT OF SHOCKED WOMAN,' yelled *The Mirror*.

I read about the children's TV presenter, Dave Benson Philips, who talked about fighting off a gull that tried to steal his sandwich at a live event in Worthing. Later, after it returned to divebomb his audience and projectile vomit onto his car, he speculated that it was a considered act of vengeance. A friend was quoted as saying. 'No one seems to know if seagulls have the capacity to harbour thoughts of revenge. But it can't be a coincidence.'

More disturbing information was uncovered in Worcester, where scientists investigating the contents of gulls' nests discovered 'roadkill and junk food' as well as 'cable ties, rubber bands and human hair.' These are the sorts of items you could expect to find in a serial killer's lair. The quaint notion of a mama bird dodging turbines to feed her chicks is considerably undermined when you picture her nest as a Jeffrey Dahmer craft project.

The story that lingered with me the most though was about a pensioner in Devon, who claimed to have been trapped in his home for six days after being repeatedly attacked by gulls and believed that it was just a matter of time before the birds committed murder.

'It might sound ridiculous, but I believe it won't be long before a baby becomes the next victim of Britain's increasingly aggressive seagulls,' he said, showing off his head wounds. 'It has led me to one brutal conclusion. We must kill the bloody things.'

The gist of his opinion was familiar to me, *when they run out of lamb's eyes, they'll come for ours*. I sent this story to my mother, hoping it'd be the one that finally turned her around to my way of thinking.

'Look,' I told her. 'This could be you.'

'Christopher wouldn't do that,' she said. 'He's my favourite son.'

But a few weeks later, while staying with Effie at our family caravan in Filey during the COVID-19 summer of 2020, I was attacked by a gull for the first time. I'd been buying fish and chips from a little hatch on the side of a chip shop on the high street when a gull swooped in and stole my dinner from my hands. Its long, stiletto beak lancing at the air near my face. The first person I told was my mother.

'Oh God!' she said. 'The little bastard. Are you okay?'

This was what I'd wanted, for her to let her guard down and drop her act. What this took was maternal concern, overriding everything. Or almost everything.

'Shit!' she said, her mistake dawning.

I laughed, having learned that, while third prize may be a kind of winning, there was no denying that first prize was the real deal and that it felt great.

'Calm down, sunshine,' she said, bristling at her loss. Not yet ready to make light of things. 'You still lost your chips. But be careful. Keep them covered up in future.'

At this point she could have meant my chips or my eyeballs, but what it really meant was that while we were still at war with the birds, my mother and I had reached an armistice.

'Alright, then,' I said.

'Alright, then,' she said.

*

While most eyes have now turned towards the sea, the gulls have been largely left to their own devices in Withernsea, protected by law as they continue to dive-bomb holidaymakers and fill their grisly nests with chunks of human scalp. Now would be the perfect time for us to have been wrong about the turbines and for them to unleash their deadly potential, but they're as benign as they've always been. As harmful as paper windmills. So, we're stuck with the gulls, growing in number, untouchable and possibly capable of bearing a grudge. We've just got to find a way to live with them. It's not the best course of action, I know, but these days, whenever the gulls show an interest in me and my chips as I stroll along the promenade, I've made it my habit to show immediate deference. To take a handful of my food and toss it their way as a sacrificial offering and a protection, hopeful that it will sate them for now and that they will remember my kindness when the revolution comes.

# Death Takes a Holiday

For a while I got hooked on a documentary series set in Blackpool called *999 What's Your Emergency?* The show follows the town's police officers, fire crews and paramedics as they take calls and hurtle towards people in need. More than the drama though, what really drew me to it was the setting. I've always been interested in TV shows that focus on seaside towns. The reasons people end up in them, what their lives are like, how they cope. I like to see how their experiences compare to mine and the people I know. Often these shows are twee and picturesque, highlighting low-stakes aspects of life by the sea. Minor dramas that focus on parish council disputes or boats that urgently need their hull's patching, lest they delay the postal delivery. But *999* was not a soft-focus, cosy view of what coastal life could be like. It was a set of cautionary reminders that, while there are wonders to be had there, a life on the coast can destroy you.

One episode had a particular focus on the lonely, isolated people, so desperate for attention and human contact that they decide to call the emergency services and report bogus problems. A feigned heart attack, a threatened suicide maybe, whatever will get someone to them soonest. This, a member of the ambulance crew tells us, is common. People whose lives have crumbled often move to the seaside in the hope of recapturing their lives when they were at their best. They remember clichés of day trips, potent sense memories. Uncomplicated, sun-soaked family times, when it was all ice cream, chips and sandcastles and they didn't know enough about the world to worry about money or relationships. With that in mind, these people up sticks and move to places like Blackpool, full of hope. But arriving in their new homes they quickly find themselves alone and isolated in towns where they have no real connections or identity, realising that all they've done is take their shitty life on a permanent holiday. And this shitty life sits beside them on the bed of their dingy, new flat and asks 'Okay, now what?'

So, when Dean Wilson told me that he'd moved to Withernsea for a fresh start after a trauma, all I could think of was 999 and what his emergency might be.

Dean and I first met in Manchester during the summer of 2019, when he was performing as part of a spoken word collective called The Hull Poets. His poems are by turns funny, sentimental and touched with longing, and on stage he is a heart-warming, captivating presence. He reads his work in a uniquely rhythmic, stuttering bark, pacing on the spot and clutching a fistful of raggedy notes at his side as if they were a security blanket. I found him hugely compelling and when we got chatting after his show and I learned that he lived in Withernsea, we arranged to meet there a few weeks later to talk about his life as the self-described 'second-best poet in town'.

Over lemon and elderflower cake in Shores Diner he gave me the rundown of his life and the reason he'd recently moved to the town. He'd already lived a few lives by that point. Had a few new beginnings. As a postman in London, a care worker at a homeless shelter in Hull and now, as a poet in Withernsea.

It was his long-term partner Kevin's death that brought Dean here. Before Kevin's terminal diagnosis with pancreatic cancer, the two of them had been looking to buy a place together somewhere along the Yorkshire coast. But that form of cancer moves fast, and time ran out for them.

'We were watching *This is England* on the telly and he said, 'I've had enough of this,' then died.' Dean pressed his knife into the cake, cutting off a small, glistening wedge. 'One minute he was alive, the next they were putting him in a body bag.'

I was taken aback by this, the way that such a painful and significant moment was just rolled out for me. It wasn't dismissive, he clearly cared about what had happened, and deeply. He just didn't see the need to garnish it with cloying sentiment. Maybe this was because it hadn't been a surprise to him. The two of them having been prepared for what would happen next. When he'd learned that he was dying, Kevin had made certain to secure Dean's future, willing him enough money to start a new life and find a place of his own to settle down.

'Before he died, he said "Dean, buy yourself a place in With." So, here I am.'

Dean is compact and stocky, with close-cropped salt and pepper hair and a bushy horseshoe moustache, giving him the appealing look of a sad and slightly tired teddy bear. It's an image that would suit someone who was inclined to wallow but despite his reasons for ending up in Withernsea, Dean's outlook on life is broadly positive.

'I've written 330 poems since I moved here,' he said, explaining that he'd never been so productive. He then handed me a carrier bag containing two of his publications, one titled 'With', his tribute to Withernsea. It's a lovingly crafted newsprint poetry pamphlet, presented in a candy-striped paper bag and filled with postcards and a miniature false moustache that matches his own. He told me he was working on his third book.

'I started writing at sixteen and published my first book at fifty-one,' he said. 'I'm fifty-four now, I could be dead tomorrow. I can't wait around.'

# Cold Fish Soup

For Dean, Withernsea is a place of familiarity and sanctuary, somewhere he has always been happy. Each day he gets up and takes a constitutional along the beach, writing poems while he walks, and, along the way, picking up pebbles that interest him. A couple of weeks before we met he'd started taking photos of these finds and posting them on his Twitter, tagging them #PebbleOfTheDay. People reacted warmly to this and responded in kind, sending him images of the pebbles they'd found on their own daily walks. One woman was so enamoured by his efforts that she embroidered an image of several of his pebbles onto a quilt and sent it to him. Whether he knows it or not, this is a real skill. To find a community without even trying and be so uncynically adept at generating positivity that he has not only been able to find it in a dying town but has also managed to transfer it onto Twitter, where good intentions generally go to die.

We finished up our cakes and I expected Dean to give me a polite goodbye, but instead he invited me along to do that day's pebble walk with him. Before we set off, we took a diversion to his home, as he'd not dressed for the unexpectedly hot weather.

'It's not far,' he said. 'I've just put too many clothes on.'

Dean's house is a neat, well-kept terrace located a couple of minutes' walk from the lighthouse where he works as a volunteer. He beckoned me into his house, a space filled with ceramic *objet d'art* and vintage furniture, the walls decorated with nautical paintings and sunburst clocks. Antimacassars are draped over the backs of G Plan easy chairs. These style choices, he told me, are based on his parents' home, the first hint I get that nostalgia is the foundation of his sense of wellbeing.

He removed his shoes and slipped into another room to change, asking if I'd mind waiting on a mat in the hall, so as not to muddy the carpets. I said that was fine and spent an enjoy-able couple of minutes admiring his thimble collection and a plaster bust of a sailor on the wall. When he returned, wearing a new shirt, he put his shoes back on then remembered some-thing he'd left in the other room.

'Bugger,' he said. 'Wait there.' Then he threw himself down on his hands and knees and briskly scuttled from sight.

I watched him go, thinking *yes, this a man who is briefly acting like a dog in order to avoid the future rigmarole of having to clean dirty footprints off his carpet, but he is also a love-able and damaged eccentric who has cultivated a world where everything has to remain 'just so' in order to maintain its precar-ious status as his sanctuary*. Whatever he told me, whatever he did, I would continue to worry about him. Whether he picked up on this I'm not sure, but he seemed especially keen to reas-sure me that he was genuinely happy.

'I feel safe here,' he told me, as we left his home and headed towards the beach. I wanted to believe that he was, that this whole town was his comfort blanket. But I struggled, because what Withernsea had taught me over and over was that people came here with bruised hearts and sound intentions, ready to save themselves, then failed.

\*

In 1992 my father had been faced with a choice: redundancy or relocation. For as long as I could remember he'd worked shifts for British Gas manning a baffling network of pipes and valves out in the otherwise flat and featureless Suffolk countryside. But when his workplace was decommissioned, a decision had to be made.

Every now and then he'd smuggle me in to work with him, so I could see what he did for a living, and I learned that this mainly involved him sitting in a chair and eating baked potatoes while staring at a bank of self-regulating pressure gauges. It seemed to me that, for most of his time there, my father could have been effectively replaced by a decent-sized rock. So, I didn't fancy his chances on the job market and was pleased when he took the relocation option. Especially as, for me, the timing couldn't have been better.

When I was much younger, I'd been trouble. I had a gang, got into fights, stole from shops. Then, just as I was starting high school, I hit puberty and got kind of flouncy. I wafted my hands when I spoke. Took to aping my mother's compelling speech patterns and mannerisms. The enthusiasm my friends showed for football, I began to show for the life and music of Prince. In short, I made a target of myself. It just took someone to notice and capitalise on it. This didn't take long. Sometime during a first term Humanities class, a kid named David opened his mouth and in doing so lit the match that would transform my high school reputation into a three-year bin fire.

'Adam touched my leg under the table!' he cried. This came from nowhere, and I don't know why he chose that moment in particular, but every face in the room swiftly oscillated in our direction. Each child recognising that something terrible was happening to someone and enjoying the thrill that this someone wasn't them.

'What?' I protested, blushing hard. 'No, I didn't!' And I hadn't, but that wasn't important.

'Yes, you did,' David said, smiling, his face glowing with the power he realised he now had. 'You fucking queer.'

Gossip quickly snowballed and I continued to loudly deny

the rumour, forgetting that to strongly react to a situation was to give it a marketing platform. If I achieved nothing else, I became a very successful brand manager for my own misery. That I'm not gay was really beside the point, what was important was that I had transformed myself into a target. And any child with a decent survival instinct will recognise the need for targets. In effect, I became a convenient smokescreen for anyone who ended up in a tricky situation. If someone found, say, their new trainers being criticised, all they needed to do was point an accusatory finger in my direction, say 'Adam's thinking about your dick!', then disappear behind a cloud of misdirection.

My friends scattered from me like dropped marbles and would begin to analyse my actions with the same level of scrutiny that tabloid columnists applied to the movements of Princess Diana. And because I was the kind of boy who referenced princesses, I made their job pretty easy. If I even looked at other boys, I was accused of checking them out. If I kept my head down, I was accused of checking out their buttocks. I tried to claw my way back into their good graces but quickly learned that broadcasting my ability to recite the lyrics to 'Raspberry Beret' was not the way to go about it. It seems that one of the only things gayer than talking about berets was conjuring up the idea of a raspberry wearing one. And the only thing gayer than that, was trying to talk to other boys about it during an interschool penalty shootout.

My problems would peak during our final year, when all pupils were asked to complete career questionnaires, detailing our traits, abilities, and interests. These were then fed into a machine that processed this information and issued a piece of paper displaying our ideal jobs. Some boys got Mechanic or Air-conditioning Engineer, others, Graphic Designer or Lifeguard. Mine said Flower Arranger, and while David's didn't say Town Crier, he did a pretty good job of making sure that everyone in school knew about it.

I took to spending most of my free time alone in my bedroom, predicting various uncertain futures. My best-case scenario being one that would end quickly, my funeral at least expertly garlanded by the friends I'd have made in the florist community. But even that seemed too far off. The sense of isolation I felt at school became oppressive and unbearable, and I'd do anything I could to avoid it. When I couldn't convince my mother that I was sick with a stomach bug or dengue fever, I found ways of making myself invisible. I learned to carry myself through school in a way that allowed me to go missing without anyone noticing, going undetected in the less popular sections of the library, where I sat concealed behind copies of *Smocks and Smocking* or *The Times Atlas of the World*. Big-format books that taught me about appearance-obscuring clothing and all the far-off places I could one day run to.

I came to learn that I was only really noticeable to teachers if I was being singled out by other children, so if the opportunity presented itself I'd slip home at lunch time and spend the afternoon hiding in my wardrobe, so as not to be detected by my parents. And here, in the dark and stillness of pretending that I was miles away sitting obediently in a physics class, I would plan ways to kill myself.

My options were limited. Out in the flatlands of Suffolk I might be lucky enough to get trampled by a bull or shot by a farmer for trespassing, but there are very few places from which I could have thrown myself. Certainly nothing with enough height to guarantee a quick and efficient death. My fear of failing at suicide and surviving was great, which also ruled out the option of hurling myself into the path of traffic or entering the garden of the rottweiler that furiously barked at me each day as I made my way to school. I didn't want to have to go through life with all of my existing problems plus the added complication of a missing arm and a face that hung from my skull in tattered pleats. I was only interested in efficient exits. I thought of overdosing, but I had no access to large volumes of pills. Shooting myself would have been perfect, but while my brother Robert owned a high-powered air pistol, I knew that he'd once shot his friend in the head with it and that this friend had remained both alive and resentful. I was still searching for a clean, failsafe off switch when the chance to move to Withernsea and leave everything behind came along. I didn't care that it came in the form of a disruptive, cost-saving initiative by British Gas, I just recognised it as a lifeline.

My father was offered several different resettlement locations across the country but moving to Withernsea had ultimately been my mother's choice.

'If you're making me leave my parents behind,' she'd said, 'then I want to live by the seaside.'

She associated resort towns with the best of things and filled our house with ornaments that reminded her of the coast. Trinket boxes decorated with varnished shells. Ornate pebbles. Vials of coloured sand. So, whether it was by nature or nurture, when it came to the move I, her water baby, was with her all the way, pro-Withernsea before I'd even looked for it on a map.

Back then, I only really knew the world through my TV, so imagined Withernsea as one of the locations in the movies and shows that I loved. Sometimes I pictured it as the town of Summer Bay from the daytime soap opera *Home and Away*.

Others it was LA County from *Baywatch* or Santa Carla in *The Lost Boys*. Places where young people could discover sex, excitement and maybe foil a vampire uprising. And then there was the sea, the amusement arcades, the drifting scent of fish and chips and fried doughnuts. There was no *999 What's Your Emergency?* back then, nothing to ruin the glamour of the place and make us wonder why the house prices were so low. Instead, we saw coastal towns as affordable paradises and wondered why everyone didn't want to live in one.

Pulling up on the seafront and stepping out of the car that first time, Withernsea seemed to be living up to its promise. The arcades lured me in instantly, the doors wide open and broadcasting a relentless soundtrack of good times, like the call to prayer of an evangelical church that was refreshingly blatant about the fact that it was only after your money. There was the clattering rush of falling coins. Casiotone gunfire. Looped bursts of disco floor-fillers. Inside, children with empty pockets lurked around the fruit machines scouring the carpets for dropped coins. The bingo offered grocery essentials as prizes. Eggs, washing powder, milk. For a full-house you could pick up a joint of gammon the size of a rugby ball. Pubs advertised entertainment every night of the week.

After my brother Ben and I had exhausted our pockets playing Moonwalker and Operation: Wolf, our family went for lunch in a café near the promenade. I took a window seat, still keen to gobble up every sight and not miss a thing. From there I could see a sun-bleached, fibreglass clown's head mounted atop a ten-foot pole outside. It had the empty, unblinking gaze of a decapitated yet still defiant enemy of state. I followed its line of sight across an exhausted-looking fairground, over the crazy golf course and past the Victorian public toilets to the remains of the old pier. And beyond them, the beach, where people of my age were hanging out. Some of them laughing in groups, some smoking in moody solitude, others sniping and hissing at each other like territorial cats. I pictured myself amongst them on warm summer evenings, playing acoustic guitar beside a fire and drawing the attention of girls, their idea of me not tainted by the mental image of my hands deftly threading a ribbon around a pink bouquet. I saw a whole new life before me then, and a small town that would save my life.

*

'Do you want to come to the indoor market?' Dean asked, after we were done on the beach. I'd told him that I'd worked there after I left university in '97, back when the building still housed the Eastgate pottery works, and he was keen to show me how it looked now.

Dean is an enthusiastic collector of Eastgate pottery and wanted me to give him intel about my time there, so I felt bad that I had nothing for him. My main job had been to hack up slabs of clay and throw them into the 'blunger' – a huge blender that churned it into gallons of liquid slip, which I then poured into plaster casts to form vases and ash trays. This is not intel, not a story. I did nothing interesting, made nothing interesting. I had small tales about the people who worked there. That the brother of the man who taught me how to trim and sponge ceramics before glazing was one of the town's two David Bowie impersonators. That I was shown how to run the slipcast production line by a man who made the national news for being fired by the Royal Mail after he was caught shoving a child into a postbag. But the majority of my time there was spent missing out. I'd returned to Withernsea after university with a painfully failed relationship behind me, a new and disabling lack of direction and that familiar urge to end it all. When a World War II bomb was discovered on Withernsea beach and destroyed in a controlled detonation I was unaware, too busy being deafened by the roar of the blunger and my thoughts of how this was not part of the bright future I'd imagined for myself.

As we made our way up the high street towards the market, Dean stopped at intervals to point out the locations of the lost sights that still live in his memory. There was the long-absent pissoir outside the old Smiles for Miles arcade. The location of a once-popular lido now replaced with a dry dock for fishing boats. He had a way of looking at these places and somehow filling in the blanks for me, projecting the ghosts of the town's architectural past. My memories were different to his, my comforts smaller. Little sparks of joy that I got from looking at the old places I knew, and of the fact that I was still alive to see them. And while it wasn't our intention, our sightseeing somehow kept returning to death.

'Two people died there the other week,' Dean said, gesturing to a pub as we made our way along the high street. 'One bloke hung himself and another just died in there. They just rented rooms and died.'

This is how it is with Withernsea. I don't know if it's a form of nominative determinism, the name of the town conjuring images of dying back and fading, of withering by the sea, but death now feels to me like it was always in the town's DNA. It could be that I'm transferring my thoughts onto it, trying to make sense of everything that happened to our family here. Making the town fit the grim narrative that I've laid over it.

That, just like in Blackpool or any other past-its-prime coastal town you might care to mention, the poverty, economic uncertainty and lack of opportunities were driving people to substance abuse and depression, then crushing them into the ground along with any hope they might have been keeping in their back pockets. I was just starting to feel bad about these thoughts, and for damning Withernsea in this way, when we passed the public toilets on Piggy Lane, where I knew that three overdosed corpses had been discovered by a cleaner one morning.

Then The Pier, the pub where I'm told that, on the night he died, my brother Robert made his way around the tables trying to sell his old tools for cash rather than turn to the rest of the family for help. And because Withernsea is small and everywhere quickly tends to lead to everywhere else it wasn't long before we were drawn to the spot where his body was found. By that point Dean and I had discussed so much death that it would have seemed oddly competitive to mention it. *I see your hanged man in a pub and raise you a dead brother.* So, we walked on by and headed for the indoor market, which felt wrong for different reasons, because whenever I was in town, I'd always made sure to stop and acknowledge the spot where Robert died.

His body had been discovered late one evening, slumped in a raised flower bed near the pier towers, a combination of over one hundred painkillers and antidepressants in his system. For a while, before the flower bed was removed, I made it a habit to sit on it myself, trying to take in the sounds and the view Robert might have had as he slipped away. It was a comfort to me to think that he would have heard the wash of the sea as he died, but little else in the surroundings felt like comfort.

Seated there, looking to my left, I could see the place where years earlier a young man had crashed his motorbike into the promenade and was hurled to his death over the sea wall. To my right, the point where one of my brother Ben's friends, agonised by a break-up, had removed all of his clothes, piled them neatly on the sea wall then leapt into the jagged rock wall below. A short walk in either direction would take me to one of the town's many nursing homes, where death is always present but moves at a steadier, less-alarming rate. This is no great surprise, really. Nothing special. I guess you can do this in any town. Death is natural after all, it's not localised to particular cursed lands, but since Robert died it has felt focussed and concentrated here. Withernsea is a small place and literally getting smaller by the day. The end is closing in. Tightening like a noose. Unless you're Dean, who finds life and joy in this town as if he's actively mining for it. But, as time passes, he seems more and more like an outlier, a remarkable exception.

'You must have stories though,' Dean said, when we reached the market and headed inside.

'Sorry?' I replied, my mind still back on the promenade.

'About working at the potteries.'

I looked around at the spaces where I once worked. Where the kilns used to be, and the banks of gutters that drained excess clay into buckets, which I'd carry over to the blunger and pour back into it. I thought of the miserable gutter-to-blunger loop that I was stuck on for eight hours a day, pausing only to drink bad coffee and think of how wonderful it would be to toss myself into the blunger and get blended in with the clay then poured into casts, my body living on in vases and ash trays. People would place flowers in me, stub cigarettes out on me.

'No, sorry,' I told him. 'I don't really have any stories.'

After Dean and I wished each other goodbye, I realised it was around midday, so I decided to grab some lunch then drive up to Spurn Point to eat it. I'd somehow never taken the journey to the very end of Spurn before but, because the weather was still hot and sunny and I had nothing pressing to do except type up my interview notes, it seemed like the time. I parked up and walked onto the sands, chewing at a sandwich and squinting past the lighthouse at the midway point, then down to the cluster of squat buildings at the end. They didn't seem too far, so I aimed for them and set off.

The surface of Spurn Point is changeable and challenging, shifting from concrete to soft sands to dunes of grass and stabbing briars, then to whole stretches of beach formed from sea-worn rubble and brick. In some areas it feels like walking on rough-hewn cobbles. At others, in the powdery white sand, almost as if I was moonwalking, my forward motion hampering my progress and somehow shifting me backwards. Two steps forward, one step back. By the time I reached the end a couple of hours later I was dehydrated, exhausted and sunburnt. I filled my water bottle from a howling, air-filled tap in the unmanned RNLI building at the point then drank from it on the beach, where I watched as a sun-addled, fully-clothed man launched himself along the sands and into the water like an excitable dog. I was considering giving this a try myself when my phone rang. It was my niece, Robert's eldest daughter, Presley.

'Have you heard?' she said.

'Heard what?'

She went on to explain that one of my brother Ben's best friends, let's call him John, had just killed himself and that Ben was in a bad way. She was going over to see him and wanted me there. The rest of my family was away on holiday and, because I was in town, I found myself designated as the responsible adult who should deal with this. I didn't feel very responsible, but I downed my water and got moving, racing back along a route that defied racing.

As I stumbled, moonwalked, back along Spurn, I thought about how little this news had stung me. How oddly convenient it was that I would be in Withernsea, writing about death, and someone would die while I was there. That's a terrible thing really, to consider a whole life lost and all the people it devastates and catch yourself thinking 'Well, this is good material.' I was concerned about how Ben was feeling, what another death of a friend would do to him and how this made me worry but, for me, the death itself felt far less than it should have. It hit me as bad news certainly, but in the way that a higher than usual utility bill might. A brief lurch of 'That's awful,' followed by a resigned 'Okay, moving on …' I was never like this when I was younger and I didn't much like the person it suggested I had grown into.

In the past, the news of a death would have rattled me at a fundamental level. After I moved permanently from Withernsea to Manchester I'd frequently call my mother so we could share the latest news and often this would include a death. She might tell me about a man in the next village who had blown himself up while dropping petrol bombs down rat holes. I would tell her about the daylight gun murder near my flat that, had I fair warning and the inclination, I could have watched from my balcony. One of us would share this sort of news and hear the other one gasp. Mouths were audibly covered in shock, muffling 'oh my Gods'. Because for us, death was still something that only really happened to criminals and the elderly.

I accept that my change in attitude is partly down to age, the growing familiarity of death the longer I live. But really, I recognised that the change in me was down to Robert. There was before his suicide, there was the immediate aftermath, then there was never being the same person again. In the same way that having a child can change you, bringing with it a new, complex and overpowering emotional range, the unexpected death of a sibling does the same. When I got the call to say that Robert had killed himself I felt somehow cored, as if a force had grabbed me by the skull and whipped my entire skeleton out of my body. I couldn't speak to explain to anyone why I had collapsed on the stairs like a fallen damsel, cradling a beeping phone in my hands. Why I was hyperventilating and couldn't stand up. This was a full set of moves that I'd have scoffed at had I seen ham actors pulling them in TV movies, but it was a reaction that certainly wouldn't have surprised David from high school. It was the same for all of us in different ways. Becky, only two years separating her and Robert, had lost her ally and her witness to her early years, and would spend the months following his death looking as if she'd lost half of the blood in her body. Or a limb. Because she kind of had. Ben, meanwhile, had appeared as if he was in a permanent state of being alternately slapped in the face and punched in the stomach. My father chose silence, because the one time I'd heard him cry was when I asked him how he felt about Robert's death and from that point on he seemed to decide that it wasn't a reaction he could countenance. What my mother felt was far beyond all of this. Incalculable and difficult to witness.

'I feel like something has been clawed out of my stomach,' she told me once, not long after Robert died. 'Like a whole chunk of me has been torn out and I can't get it back to fill the hole.'

She didn't say this through tears. Her words were almost robotic. Grey-toned. The slow and contained manner of someone using all of their will to hold themselves together. Of talking while gravely wounded. And there I was walking along Spurn, regarding someone else's grief, someone else's world collapsing, and thinking of how it benefited me. How convenient it was. Wondering how to structure it. *Do I open up the essay with this or leave it until later?*

I phoned Presley back, wanting to undo the poison of this thought.

'Does he need anything?' I asked. 'I can pick him up whatever he wants. Fags? Beer?'

I heard her call into the living room and Ben's murmured, bassy response.

'He just wants orange juice,' she said.

In the end I picked him up some chocolate too, trying to tap into what I knew had made him happy as a child, because I realised that I didn't really know him that well as an adult. As a kid he'd always wanted volume. Mass. The biggest of things. So, I went to Tesco and bought a huge carton of Tropicana and a bar of Dairy Milk the size of a comic book, then drove over to see him.

Presley opened the door and pulled me in for a deep hug then led me into the living room, where Ben was sitting on the sofa with his friend, Matty. The two of them looked ravaged, as if they'd been up all night, which I'd come to learn they had. We exchanged subdued greetings then all four of us headed through to the kitchen for coffee. I watched Presley as she began fussing with mugs, wondering how she felt about all this. She's a helper, so won't make things about herself, but she must have been thinking about her dad. I wanted to ask her if she was okay, but I felt awkward about it, concerned that this might break any spell she was using to hold herself together. In truth, this was something I wouldn't tell myself until much later, trying to feel better about how useless and ineffectual I'd been. Instead, trapped in that moment, I'd just handed Ben the juice and the chocolate.

'Cheers,' he said, tearing them open immediately and consuming them wildly, like a hungry bear who'd stolen a picnic. He glugged heavily from the carton, bit a chunk from the Dairy Milk as if it were a chicken leg, then leaned back against the kitchen counter and began explaining what had happened to John.

His words were bellowed, as if he was aiming them to the cheap seats rather than at me, two feet away from him. I don't know if it was adrenaline or shock that caused it, but he was all volume, his mouth churning the chocolate and blasting candy-sweet morning breath into the room. I stood there, inhaling this and wincing at what I was hearing. The specifics. The awfulness of it. I looked to Presley, who had picked up a mug and was cradling it against her chest as if it was a newborn kitten, her eyes directed to the floor. Finally, when Ben was done, when every detail was out of his system, he let out a long sigh, punctuated by quiet, exhausted swears.

'... fucking hell ... shit.'

It was clear that he couldn't believe this was happening to him again. Why people kept dying for no good reason. For him, early death was supposed to come from things like cancer or a car crash. A circumstance that turns up and takes you away. You don't take yourself away, that's just madness. I think what he found the hardest though was how hard he'd tried to stop it from happening.

'I've not slept,' he said, taking another bite of chocolate and explaining how John had arrived at the house in distress the previous night. He and Matty had realised something was seriously wrong, that John was beyond upset. He wouldn't stop apologising, telling them that he didn't deserve to live. So, they did all the things you're supposed to do. Stayed up talking to him, listening, watching him closely and guiding him away from danger, from the kitchen and the knife block. Keeping John safe until they his parents came to take him home where, not long after, he would die.

'He kept shaying shorrry …' Ben said, shoving a disabling amount of chocolate into his mouth while he spoke, so Matty took over.

'I told him "You don't need to apologise. We love you, mate." But it wasn't enough.'

It was disarming to hear this sort of thing from one of Ben's friends, a group of people I'd always thought of judgementally and in two dimensions. Lads he went drinking with when he was supposed to be at family events or turning up for work. So, I didn't expect to hear one of them being sensitive and emotional, talking openly about the deep bonds of fraternal love.

We took our coffees back into the living room, Presley holding back to tidy the kitchen, Ben and Matty returning to their positions on the sofa, exhausted from lack of sleep and having tried their best to save their friend. We made for quite a scene, the three of us. Ben, sticky with chocolate, looking slapped once again. Matty drained and vacant. And me, the piece of shit who, even as I chastised myself, was working out how I'd write about it.

*

When I was looking to kill myself back in '97 I found that Withernsea offered as few options as Suffolk. It was a new experience for me to be looking at the landscape in this way. It had once represented nothing but hope and now, having returned from university under one of my dark and heavy clouds, I found myself assessing its deadly potential wherever I looked. While the cliffs were perilous, I would have had to have been pretty determined to use them for suicide, really needing to pick my spot. Erosion has gnawed them back to something higher and more precarious these days, but in the '90s they were low, grassy and soft, largely overlooking sand rather than rocks. Perhaps if I were looking to cash in on an insurance policy by breaking a limb or two and was after something less risky than a flight of stairs, I would have found my place. But as a way to check out permanently, it was a non-starter. Still, I spent a lot of time on the cliffs, waiting. For what, I don't know. Inspiration, maybe. Perhaps a sense of calm.

The few bodies that were found at the foot of these cliffs tended to come from the sea. Washed up alongside the refuse and the wadded lumps of raw sewage masquerading as pitch-black pebbles. They generally belonged to people with a mental illness, who had wandered off on their own and been trapped by rapid tides or killed themselves elsewhere only to be discovered on the sands by an unfortunate dog walker. It's no more common in Withernsea than it is in the rest of Holderness, or anywhere on the UK coast for that matter, but still, start Googling 'Withernsea' and 'body found' is one of the first things that autofills.

If I'd been truly determined, I could have found a way to do it. Thrown myself off the lighthouse maybe. Hired a room in a pub and hung myself from a beam. Then there was the sea, which there's a romance to, I guess. Of wading into the waters that had been my solace for so many years and never coming out of them again. The longer I stared at the sea and considered my fate, the more it stopped looking like my own private waterpark and began to resemble a huge compressing muscle, draped in a gossamer-thin membrane. I thought of finally giving myself over to it and being taken down deep. Allowing it all inside me, flooding my lungs. Being spun. Crushed by the pressures. Dashed against the rocks until I was as tender and bloody as a fillet steak before being deposited back onto the beach, my insides home to a community of burrowing worms. But I could never do that. Being at the edge of the land, the end of the world, forces you to make a decision and the one I made was the one I judged other people for; I picked another place to live and I ran. Robert though, had always been less afraid of consequences than me. So, he stood at the end of the world and embraced it.

\*

Robert was everything I thought I wanted to be. He had long hair and a leather jacket. He drank and smoked. Rode a motorbike, played electric guitar and had girls in his room. It sometimes seems less like he died and more as if Hollywood just stopped writing him. And he defined the standard of what I thought it was to be a man. A standard that, as I grew older, I found myself incapable of living up to. Never having his confidence or self-belief. So, in lieu of stories of my own, I'd often talk to people of Robert, my eyes starry with wonder as if I were regaling my audience with fantastical folk tales about a valiant and daring hero.

'He has a chipped tooth because he got in a street fight and someone hit him with a padlock on a chain!'

'He has five girlfriends and none of them knows!'

'He can drink ten pints and still play "Sunshine of Your Love" on his guitar! His guitar is really cool! It's a white Stratocaster and has a skull painted on it! No, no, he won't let me touch it.'

By the time our family made the move to Withernsea, Robert had already moved out of the family home and had a place of his own in Haverhill. A job, a girlfriend, a daughter, a life. So, we left him behind and began building our new world in Yorkshire. I'd go back to Suffolk and visit him every so often and he'd take me around pubs, teaching me how to drink and explaining how to chat up women. To me in Withernsea, bobbing about in the sea and trying to work things out, it had seemed like Robert had it made back in Haverhill. All of the pieces of the puzzle firmly in place. Then, without much warning he arrived in Withernsea with Presley in tow; lost, broken and ready to start again. Like me, he was after a clean slate but also a life defined once again by his rules. New pubs, new women, new experiences. He was ready to rebuild his empire in the North.

For a while, until he found a job and his own place, he and Presley moved in with us. She took the spare room, while Robert slept on a fold-up bed in the dining room. His domain reduced to an uncomfortable, six-foot by four-foot rectangle beside the dresser. He'd pack it all up each morning before the rest of the family awoke so as not to feel as if he was in the way. He knew it was temporary, but it clearly hurt him to recognise his lot, to be so profoundly aware that the life he'd cultivated and controlled had reached this low point. And in that room, over the days and weeks, I watched him change. Saw the bags grow under his eyes. The consequences of this fresh start hitting home. His plans of swaggering into a new town, his notions of a clean slate, none of it was running smoothly and it rocked him. I didn't know what to do with this version of him, this fallen, less cocksure Robert. He reminded me of me, and I found that unsettling. Disappointing. So, when I could, I avoided him, trusting in his resourcefulness and hoping that he'd find his way back to his old self before too long.

One evening, a month or so after he'd moved in with us, I came home late from a concert in Hull, creeping into the house so as not to wake anyone. Ben and my parents were already asleep but I could see that the light was on in the dining room, which meant that Robert was awake, as he usually was when I arrived home in the early hours. I heard the squeak and groan of his bed as he rolled out of it to shamble into the doorway, where he stood looking drawn and haggard.

'Hey,' I said. 'How are you doing?'

I knew the answer and I didn't want to hear it, so I was pleased with the false answer he gave me.

'Good,' he said. 'Tell me about tonight.'

We fell into conversation then, the one we'd often have when I'd return home late. While I puggled my ear with my finger, trying to recover from whistling tinnitus, he'd ask me about the band I'd seen. If I'd pulled a girl. How much I'd had to drink. I always enjoyed this, the interest he showed in me and my life, so rather than give in to exhaustion or booziness, I'd settle into the conversation. Telling him the small details that seemed important back then, and he did the same, but from a point of nostalgia. The things he'd done when he was my age. I made us each a mug of tea and had just set them down on the dining table, ready to enjoy the chat, when he lunged at me. It was my reflex to flinch, my physical contact with Robert having mostly been related to violence. An unexpected punch from a fist bearing a studded wristband or his pewter, bald eagle ring. Feel the sudden sensation of being thrown to the floor, twisted into a painful shape and made to submit. The flash of a flick-knife near my eye, just to watch my reaction. I don't really know how I normalised this, how I compartmentalised it, as if he were the main character in a 1970s sitcom called *That's just Robert!*, about a guy who had a number of worrying traits that we all forgave because he was familiar to us and had a few good lines. But none of that mattered then because what he'd wanted was comfort.

He hugged me tightly, sobbing into my shoulder, huge heaving clucks of grief for what he'd lost and what his life had become. The things he was missing, details of which emerged in a series of choked, cracked statements.

'I just want to … get drunk … have a fight … and … and fuck women.'

This outburst seemed to come from the realisation that he'd lost so much status that he was now reduced to living vicariously through me and my small experiences. And it was strange to be holding him like that, as I'd never really hugged a man before. Least of all Robert, whom I had never known to seek affection, let alone succumb to it. I still expected him to turn on me, the way a cat sometimes will, happily purring on your lap before, without warning or justification, scratching the absolute shit out of you. So, I waited for the gut punch, Robert's sudden and violent awareness of his vulnerability. Instead, he let himself fall into me and I felt his hard, sinewy body bucking against mine, pulling in for support. I realised then how much bigger than him I was; how much bigger I'd been for a long time. He'd loomed so large as a presence, as a *big* brother, that I hadn't realised I'd grown to tower above him. It was confusing to feel such a big dynamic shift, this reversal, to be forced to recognise the size and shape of him and that there was a part of Robert that could allow itself to be frail.

Forced to compare me and Robert and asked to place a bet on which one of us would check out early, most people who knew us would have put their money on me. But I'm here and he's not. It's not strength exactly, nothing to do with that really. I'm not better or braver than Robert for not succumbing to the need to make it all stop. I've rolled the idea around enough at this point that I often feel it's the opposite and that it completely fits in with our personalities that he'd be the one to leave while I would remain, growing older now than he ever was. He was the one who would jump onto a motorbike without a helmet and pop wheelies, who ran towards peril with clenched fists and a fearless heart. Whereas I winced at potential outcomes and calculated risk, rarely jumping into anything unknown. So, it makes total sense that he would say 'Fuck this, I'm going in' then throw himself into death without concern for the darkness or the aftermath, and why I would choose to stick around.

\*

The last time I saw Robert I was visiting his house during a trip home around Christmas. It was a dozen or so years after he'd moved to Withernsea and he was married by then, with six children all crammed into his three-bedroom house. There was nowhere in his home that you could rest your gaze without seeing a broken, candy-coloured toy or a child wearing a chocolate-smear smile. And in the middle of it all sat Robert, gently swivelling in an office chair beside his computer, engulfed by a fug of cigarette smoke and looking as if he'd just returned from an hour spent extricating himself from an electric fence. His eyes were wide and raw, staring out from a pale, pillowy head. His hair stood wildly on end. Something crucial was missing from his face.

'What happened to your eyebrows?' I asked, speaking, I realised, to his forehead.He lifted his hand to the void where his eyebrows had once been and absently rubbed the skin. 'Scratched 'em off,' he said casually, then smiled. His face crumpled into a sudden chaos of lines. It easily aged him by twenty years.

Like a bad wig, once you've noticed that someone has no eyebrows you can concentrate on little else, so I said the first thing that occurred to me.

'I guess you could draw some on.'

He smiled weakly and playfully told me to fuck off then turned to his computer and began pecking at his keyboard. It was a disappointing reaction. Had I spoken to Robert like that during his peak in the late 1980s he'd have pounced on me and drawn a set of angry eyebrows on my face with a jumbo marker. And maybe a Hitler moustache. He wasn't one to let things slide. He'd always been a man of high emotion. Had lived and reacted big. And I had learnt from him.

His examples and behaviour had shown me what to do and what not to do. They revealed the mysteries of the world. He taught me how much alcohol is too much. What a clitoris was and where. How to gut a fish with a saw-backed hunting knife and why I would never want to. I learned about music, drugs, fear and pain. That I don't like horror films. That I like pro-wrestling. That farts are funny if you light them and funnier still when they set fire to your trousers. That older brothers' bedrooms contain magazines featuring naked women that will flip a switch in your midsection that can never be turned off. He showed me what it was like to be held down and farted upon. To be punched. To have an axe thrown at me twice during a camping trip that we never spoke of again. How to swear. To shoot an air gun. To play 'Smoke on the Water' on the guitar. And eventually, what it was like to love your brother harder than he knew and have him become a stranger.

If I had known at that point that he had already tried to kill himself a number of times, that he'd had the same thoughts in Withernsea as me, we might have had a more significant conversation. Had I been told of the night that he'd staggered into the sea and tried to drown himself or of the time he'd overdosed and woken up cursing that he was still alive, I'm sure I would have said more. I'd have at least tried to find out what drove him to scratch off his eyebrows. But looking at his living room, the chaos of it, I'd guessed at stress rather than suicidal ideation. So, I just made small talk about the weather and his dust-caked shelf of Iron Maiden collectibles then drove back to Manchester, my job done. My brother successfully visited. A box ticked.

A few months later, Robert's body would be discovered on the promenade. The men who found him had been returning from the pub and thought at first that he was a sleeping drunk, so relaxed and reclined did he look. It was just after Easter and unusually cold. Parts of the country had been hit with deep snows and over in Manchester my daughter Effie and I had celebrated Easter Sunday with the building of a snowman. Aware that a rough sleeper could catch their death in weather like this, especially on the promenade, where the icy wind cuts like razors, the men tried to rouse Robert and quickly realised that it was too late. Later, after his autopsy and the discovery of the drugs in his system, Robert's death would be ruled as misadventure. This made it sound like a mishap. An oopsy. But to me there was no doubt it was certain and determined. No mistake.

*

When we were much younger, Robert and I would watch the wrestling together. I'd had a friend who would tape-record WWF events for me off Sky TV and these shows were one of the few things that Robert would happily sit down and watch with me. One of his favourite wrestlers was a huge guy named Kerry Von Erich, 'The Texas Tornado'. When he appeared on the screen Robert would sit forward in his chair, waiting for The Tornado Punch, which involved Von Erich spinning across the ring as if throwing a discus then punching his opponent in the head. They would react as if the blow had almost decapitated them, backflipping then lying motionless on the canvas, ready to be pinned. Even as a kid I struggled to find this convincing, but Robert loved it. Enjoyed the way that Von Erich celebrated his wins by staggering around the ring, head banging like a stoner at a Metallica concert. I could never quite understand the appeal if I'm honest. While Von Erich had long flowing hair and the body of Hercules, he was also cursed with a face that bore a permanent look of bucktoothed confusion, like a cartoon mule being forced to complete an algebra test. But after Robert died, I often found myself thinking seriously about Kerry Von Erich.

Beyond his looks and goofy moves he was largely famous for being one of the six sons of the Von Erich family, who ran and competed in a successful wrestling promotion in Dallas, Texas during the 1980s. What these brothers were largely famous for though, more than any of their other achievements, was dying. The first two deaths were accidental, Jack in childhood from drowning then David, the eldest, from diverticulitis or an accidental drug overdose, depending on who you speak to. But the following three deaths, of Kerry, Mike and Chris, were all from suicide. Kevin, the sole surviving brother, now lives by the sea in Hawaii, where he tries to find a sense of peace after all of his losses. 'Once I had five brothers,' he says, 'now I'm not even a brother.'

In the aftermath of Robert's death I would wonder a lot about how the Von Erich brothers could do that to their parents, to each other, and the children they left behind. I struggled to understand how each of them intimately knew the impact of death and what it would do to their loved ones, then killed themselves anyway. The answer to this is obvious; they felt they had no other choice. But for me, for my family, there is no longer a concept of choice.

I'd always thought that, if it came to it, I could have got away with committing suicide, having trained myself to feel unimportant. A spare child. One of four kids and crucially the one who, for the most part, didn't cause a fuss and avoided getting in the way. If I died the order would still be the same. My brothers would still be brothers, the eldest and the youngest remaining unchanged, my sister still a sister. It didn't feel like my passing would disrupt anything. Then Robert died and it felt like he had used up our family's one free early-death-pass. We all absorbed the impact of his passing, the repercussions of it, and knew that this was no longer an option for the rest of us. We were each branded by his death, marked for life.

# Death Takes a Holiday

Once I had a big brother, now I am the big brother, and that's how it must remain. There could be no checking out early, no escape for any of us. No deadly swan dives. No wading into the sea. If we were going to insist on standing here at the end of the world, there was no embracing it. We had to keep stepping back from the ever-approaching edge and hold each other fast.

# There Is a Light That Never Goes Out

'Have you seen the news?' my mother asked, WhatsApping me a link to a BBC News report about Withernsea Lighthouse. It explained how, in July of 1976, it had been decided there was no use for it anymore and its bulb had been turned off for the final time. But after forty-four years of inactivity, and in response to the COVID-19 pandemic, there had been a change of heart.

When I consider a lighthouse I picture a candy-striped tower situated on a rocky spur, its beam illuminating dark and turbulent waters while waves lash and batter its walls. Withernsea's, though, is set back a quarter mile from the beach, a giant white pepper mill surrounded by residential buildings and convenience stores. Visible from miles around, it is the town's one distinguishing mark, so when you finally stand in front of it and discover that it's flanked by terraced houses you feel a little tricked. As if it never had a purpose at all and if you looked behind it you'd discover it was just a cardboard cut-out propped up against a stand. The lighthouse's distance from the coast, so far away it can't possibly have served any practical use, certainly suggests that nobody ever had any real faith in it. Its presence is so obviously wrong, so uniquely unnecessary, it's hard to shake the feeling that it was both designed and built with a light that was always destined to be extinguished.

Since the late 1980s Withernsea Lighthouse has performed many roles. Enter it and turn to your left, heading into the base of the tower, you will find yourself in an RNLI museum crammed with nautical curios and leggy fashion mannequins dressed up to resemble distinguished lifeboat men. Turn to your right and you will find an exhibit dedicated to the life of Kay Kendall, a Withernsea-born actor who starred in the film *Genevieve* and became Rex Harrison's third wife before dying of leukaemia in 1959. Head through that and you'll find a café and a large garden, where outdoor plays are often performed by the local amateur dramatics' society and where once, for a charity abseil, my brother Robert landed, having just descended the 127-foot tower dressed as Gary Glitter. In essence, Withernsea Lighthouse has become the architectural equivalent of a defective Swiss Army knife, capable of performing any function the town requires apart from the one it was created for. Then came 2020, when it was decided that its lamp would shine once again and continue to blaze until the pandemic was over. The BBC report featured an interview with Lyndsey Jones, the lighthouse manager, who put great faith in the value of the gesture.

'I think it has given people a bit of reassurance,' she said. 'People of Withernsea have referred to it as their "Beacon of Hope".'

Later that day I phoned my friend Zoe for one of our regular lockdown check-in calls. I began telling her about the news report then stopped myself, remembering that, thanks to me, she has come to hate Withernsea Lighthouse. On trips to the town together we somehow always end up there and once inside I will become gripped by a compulsion to climb each of the 144 internal steps and reach the viewing platform at the top, which offers a 360-degree view of the town and of the broader Holderness coast. Each time a visitor reaches this point they receive an A5 certificate of achievement, and I now have so many that I could easily paper a downstairs bathroom with them. Fearful of heights, Zoe always declines the trip to the top, choosing instead to dutifully wait at the bottom of the stairs amongst the museum exhibits of dead-eyed figures and displays of sea-worn artefacts, queasily looking up at me as I ascend.

'It's weird,' I told her, trying to move the subject away from the building itself, 'because, at the exact moment when they switched off that lamp in 1976, I nearly died.'

I was playing with the timeline a little here, adjusting it to fit the narrative, but give or take a few hours it was true. I was just a couple of months old at the time and had been on holiday with my family in Scotland. From what I understand, my parents had dozed off, leaving me lying helpless in my pram and exposed to the full power of the sun. On any other year in Scotland, I might have been at a greater risk of drowning from rainfall, but the summer of '76 was one of the hottest on record, a time when a new-born baby left outside without the shelter of a parasol could be roasted to perfection in a matter of minutes. By the time my mother responded to my cries I was beet-red and had puffed up like a bag of microwave popcorn. My temperature hit the forties and she became convinced that I was done for. When my mother and I talk about it now, she's flippant and blasé, recalling the situation as if she were repeating an anecdote about an overcooked chicken. At the time though, she'd been inconsolable, wrapping me up in damp towels and holding me to her breast, howling, convinced that God had plans for me.

'I thought that the angels had come to take you to heaven,' she used to tell me. 'Because you were too beautiful to live.'

Had she known of Withernsea back then and learned that its lighthouse was being decommissioned, she'd have no doubt seen a deep significance in the timing. The light that went out in the tower would also inevitably go out in me, her sweet, cherubic boy.

'Well,' Zoe said, when I was finally done talking. 'It's nice to see how you've taken a global pandemic and found a way to make it all about you.'

'No,' I said, protesting. 'Not at all, I just thought it was funny that she said I was beautiful. You know what I looked like when I was a baby, I'd have let me burn too.'

It was a weak defence though, and both of us knew it. Yes, I was a hideous-looking child, all chicken feather hair and a dazed resting expression that suggested my parents had spent a great deal of my infancy handling me like a hot potato, but Zoe and I have been friends since birth and if there's one thing she knows it's my bad habits. This is one of my worst and I confess that I do it all the time: hear people's stories and somehow snake them back to me and one of my own. Someone might tell me that their pet has died and, once I've got the obligatory sympathies out of the way, I'll find a way to pull things back around to me.

'God, it was the same with my old cat Sam,' I'll say, my words bubbling with overcooked emotion. 'As the drugs hit his system, he looked me straight in the eyes as if to say "Why?" then he went limp … and died.'

It's an ugly habit I know, made especially so during a global crisis, when millions have died from the virus. There was no angle where I could truly justify guiding the story back to me, unless I caught COVID-19 myself and survived, at which point, oh boy, would I have a story. But lacking the brazen artifice to fake a persistent cough and claim that I *do* have the virus and that this *is* all about me actually, I tried instead to lead the conversation in yet another direction. Away from my embarrassment and over to the broader issue of my concern for Withernsea in the face of a COVID-19-triggered economic downturn. Another looming death.

'I don't know how it'll survive all this,' I said, and this time my concern was genuine and heartfelt.

\*

When I first visited Withernsea almost thirty years ago, it was already in the process of slowly and defiantly falling to its knees. While it possessed some radiation of the charm it had back in its heyday, the high street still buzzing with tourists and lit by the glow of plastic buckets and spades, it was very much in its decline. I didn't realise this at the time, too hopped-up on the thrill of new beginnings and impressed by everything I encountered there. Having never known what a seaside town with money was supposed to look like, Withernsea glimmered with the promise of better things.

It had once been a thriving resort town, the train network delivering thousands of Yorkshire holidaymakers over to its shores each week. Look at photos of the town back in the early part of the twentieth century, or at the rail tourism posters painted by Albert Lambart or Maud Briby, and it could easily be mistaken for the set of a BBC costume drama. Well-dressed families were depicted swanning along the promenade. Flapper girls perched upon the groynes or lay supine on the sands, shading themselves with Japanese parasols. But things started to change in 1961, when the head of British Railways, Dr Beeching, revised the branch rail network and pruned the route to Withernsea, deeming it not profitable or popular enough, the signs of atrophy quickly began to show. Lack of footfall led to the exit of anything grand and the town went from flourishing to surviving. Businesses went under, the fine houses and hotels became old folks' homes or were portioned up into low-cost flats and the town stopped being a place that people painted pictures of.

Many here are still resentful about the demise of the trains. When I'd mentioned them to James from the lighthouse a few months before lockdown he'd informed me that 10,000 people had visited by rail across the fortnight before the line closed. 'Does that sound unviable to you?' he'd said, his words burning with a fire that made me feel as if, not only had the network closed down the day before, but that I had been personally responsible. This strength of feeling wasn't new to me though, it was how I'd first learned of the existence of Dr Beeching. On November 5th, sometime during the mid-'90s, a few of the locals chose to demonstrate their ability to bear a grudge, crafting an effigy of Beeching and setting fire to it before pushing it out to sea. A group of us gathered to watch it bobbing in the water, sputtering and smoking as it floated away.

'Who's that supposed to be?' I asked a woman next to me.

'Dr Beeching,' she said, adjusting her scarf.

'Why are they burning him? What did he do?'

'He killed the trains.'

In doing so, Beeching almost killed the town as well, removing a vital tourist route and kicking off an economic decline from which it will likely never fully recover. Withernsea now exists on a knife edge, and the arrival of the pandemic risks removing that knife entirely, transforming it into a holiday destination marketable only to people who slow down for car crashes. The Hull University Teaching Hospitals NHS Trust is so aware of this that they recently launched a campaign urging people to move to the region, using the slogan 'God's own county. Tucked away in the naughty corner'. It's an odd angle to take but not without justification. There is a sense that, for some reason, this part of the country is being punished and always will be.

In my lifetime, several of the town's flagship businesses have closed down. Eastgate Potteries, which had been operating since the 1950s, fell foul of the decline in UK manufacturing not long after I'd stopped working there in the late '90s. Proudfoots supermarket, where I'd got my first job back in '93, stacking shelves and operating a huge rubbish compactor next to the chiller, had closed down too, the site now split between an Aldi and a Poundstretcher. Teddy's Nightclub, a staple of the entertainment scene, underwent so many reinventions that it essentially disintegrated. A shed-like cabaret bar and entertainment complex, Teddy's rested on the promenade, its rump exposed to the waves and the marquee above the door boasting 'The Place to be in Withernsea' and 'The No.1 Nightclub in the North'. Words that reached for something but in reality meant that it was the one place in town where you might get to see Bernard Manning or Alvin Stardust perform. It went through a few changes over the years and briefly changed its name to The G Spot, which is how it appeared in the background of my sister's wedding photos, peeking over the wall of the ornamental flower garden where they held their shoot.

'The G Spot's going out of business,' people said, laughing, 'because no one can find it.'

Then it went out of business and people laughed some more. When it burned down and collapsed into the sea people laughed in a different, bleaker way. The empty plot where it once stood is now surrounded by a border of huge fence panels, each plastered with a large black and white image showing Withernsea back when it was thriving. Scenes of packed beaches and grinning figures in Edwardian dress encouraging passers-by to consider the good old days and not the crumbling and neglected foundations that they conceal. It's the equivalent of an actor circulating a twenty-year-old headshot, and no one is fooled.

The one stable part of the local economy is still the arcades – a series of interconnected warehouse sized buildings that run back-to-back with the high street, their doors wide open, broadcasting the clatter of the penny falls and the blare of video games across the valley gardens and over towards the promenade. The locals know the arcades as 'The Muggies', either because they mug you of your money or because 'only the mugs use them'. It depends on who you talk to. But even during a recession they are a draw. I once took a girlfriend to them and tried to win her a plush Hello Kitty from a crane grabber machine. After a few failed attempts, I managed to snag one and hoist it upwards, but just as it was about to drop down the chute and into my girlfriend's waiting hands, the claw spasmed and opened up, releasing the toy back into the pit of Kitties. I called a member of staff over to tell her what had happened and she just laughed at me.

'Of course it did,' she told me. 'It's rigged.'

'That doesn't seem fair.'

'It isn't,' she said, gesturing to the dozens of flashing machines around her. 'But how do you think they pay for this place?'

She walked away and I headed back to the machine, pushing another coin into the slot thinking *Fuck you, I'll show you rigged*. Not knowing quite what I meant but determined to beat the system and impress a woman with my ability to eventually spend £25 on winning her a cat-shaped stocking stuffed with seven pence worth of shredded medical gauze.

But whatever I think of them, to see the arcades in 2020, all shuttered and silent, their flashing lights switched off, is to consider the town without a pulse.

A lot of the local hope around regenerating Withernsea and turning around its fortunes, has been placed in the construction of a new pier. The town's original one was opened in 1878 and in exchange for one penny, tourists were offered the opportunity to walk to the end and experience what it was like to stand 1,196 feet out into the North Sea. Then someone obviously thought, 'Hey, maybe we should build a lighthouse to make sure no one crashes into this thing.' But by the time that was built the pier had been almost totally destroyed by a series of storms and nautical calamities, several ships having blundered through its iron girders, whittling it back until only the crenelated stone entrance remained. Walking out that far into the sea is now the sole reserve of suicidal waders and wildly optimistic pearl divers, neither of whom make for appealing faces of a tourism campaign.

The proposed new pier would be half the length of the original and feature a two-story restaurant and renewable energy centre, fitted with solar panels, wind turbines and a hydro-electric generator. The architects rendering looks modern, appealing and forward-thinking, which of course means that funding for it has been refused by the Rural Development Programme for England, who stated that the project doesn't meet with national priorities. But when I read a newspaper interview with Torkel Larsen, the head of the Withernsea Pier and Promenade Association, he still seemed pretty chipper and positive about the whole thing.

'The upside is we do have everything in place. The only thing we haven't got is the money.'

This is as close to an honest town slogan as it's possible for Withernsea to get, with 'doesn't meet with national priorities' pulling a close second. It's certainly preferable to the unofficial one I most commonly hear when I tell Yorkshire folk where I'm from.

'Withernsea is a shithole,' they'll say, and I'll immediately go into defence mode, as if I were standing up for a feeble friend who was being kicked by a bully. I mentioned this to Zoe, hating the idea that my town was always being beaten while it was down.

'But it is a bit shit though isn't it?' she said.

'No, it not. It's just …' I fumbled for a word and she let me hang there for a while before chipping in.

'Shit?' she said.

'I was going to say "tired", but yeah, okay,' I said. 'I just didn't want anyone else to say it.'

After we got off the phone, I felt a bit uncomfortable. As if I'd betrayed Withernsea by admitting that it was flawed. So, I messaged my mother, asking her how the town was getting on, wanting to know if she'd heard anything. She was typically positive and dismissive of my concerns.

'It will be fine,' she said, her message followed by a string of smiley face emojis and a GIF of a dancing dog.

'How though?' I said, pushing. Not wanting the soft response and knowing that my mother's default setting is optimism. 'How can it be fine?'

'I've been talking to the angels. ☺☺☺'

'What have you been asking for?'

'For it all to be ok soon,' she said. 'They always do what I ask. You have to repeat your request three times. It works for all sorts of things.'

It's true that my mother asks the angels for everything. For spaces in busy car parks, for her favourite performers to win on *The Voice*, for sunburned babies to survive to adulthood, and now she is asking for Withernsea to get through all this.

'The Government,' she said, 'doesn't care about Withernsea at all, but the seaside angels do.'

All this talk of angels gave me the in that I needed, allowing me to talk about the thing I was really worried about.

'I'm worried about Dad getting the virus.'

'He won't,' she said. 'Don't worry. The angels are on it!'

My father's health hasn't been something I've liked to bring up too often during the pandemic, not wanting my mother to dwell on his vulnerability too often. But as days and weeks lost their form and meaning, one of the ways I've have kept track of time is through my father, whose life expectancy I am in the process of measuring out based on the various diagnoses of his ailments.

'He has Type 2 diabetes, advanced kidney disease, myeloma and he needs a heart bypass,' I tell people, airily counting off his disorders on my fingers and making light of them because to do anything else would be unbearable. 'Oh, and he's going deaf too, but I don't think that's fatal.'

I'm doing the maths. Factoring in the cumulative impact of his illnesses and how they might come to affect the time he has remaining. We've already been given a ballpark figure for the myeloma. When my parents got the letter from the hospital confirming how much time he likely has left, my mother phoned me up to break the news.

'It says we have forty months,' she told me. 'Mind you, it took a month for the letter to arrive, so I suppose we have thirty-nine now.'

We both laughed at this, then fell into the small silence of feeling bad about it. And if she's as like me as I think she is, we would have both been using that time to think about the 'we' in her statement. It's not just my father, it's all of us, working out how much time we have left with him and how to capitalise on it when, thanks to lockdown, our mother is the only person who is allowed to see him.

His catalogue of illnesses had put him in a severely at risk group and soon after the announcement of lockdown his doctor advised him to shield himself from the public, adding that he'd be guaranteed a bed in the event that his life became threatened by the virus. By that point though, he was long used to having his life threatened and soon saw the upside in a government mandate for him to stay at home and watch TV without being chastised for idleness.

'It's not easy,' he said when I phoned him up on Father's Day, a smile in his voice, 'but I'm coping somehow.'

This was followed by a crinkling noise, which I recognised as the sound of him opening a packet of biscuits and shoving his fist inside it. This in turn was followed by the sharp crackle of my mother snatching the packet away from him.

'Ian!' she barked. 'Diabetes!'

She scolds him like a dog, but he needs it. Left to his own devices he would eat himself into a coma. Despite the knowledge that his blood sugar alone is enough to kill him, he still cram-eats sugary snacks whenever he can. He conceals cakes from my mother in the same way teenagers hide cigarettes from disapproving adults, the lit tip held inward towards the palm, shielded by the shell of the hand. Except with my father, who has never smoked, the cigarette is replaced with an individual fruit pie or a Cadbury's mini roll.

'Is that a fondant fancy?' my mother will ask, and he'll lower his head in shame then hand it over.

'It was just one.'

'Yeah, well it might as well be one cyanide pill.'

We use the language of death and suicide flippantly, like it doesn't scare us. If we took it seriously, we might have to stop and think of Robert and of how we were all too late to save him. So, we joke, look on the bright side, talk to angels, chastise each other and make light as if we're not fearful.

'If you think I'm living here with your ghost,' she tells my father, 'then I've got a shock for you, mister.'

Because she doesn't leave the house anymore, my mother is always there to police my father. This is her job now and there is a large part of me that feels mad about this. That she always had to dedicate herself to looking after a man who doesn't seem inclined to look after himself. And beyond that, she has a set of kids who can't fend for themselves either and collapse into helplessness at the first whiff of drama. It's tough at these times to remember that I'm one of them and as much a part of the problem as any of us. In that sense there's something to be said for my parents' quarantine. Before the virus our mother had to look out for all of us, her stumbling, mewling brood, but now, locked down with my father, he's the only one of us she has to protect because he's the only one she can.

Despite being the most at-risk person I know, and having his every movement monitored, my father has taken to quarantine better than most. Within a few weeks of lockdown most people I knew had started to appear on Zoom chats looking as if they'd spent three weeks handcuffed to a radiator. Not long after that they would start to make out that their webcams were broken. Vanity was dying, the pace of life was slowing, and people would have to adjust. My father though, was made for this life, and it's one way that we've found some common ground.

My father and I have never been super close. We've never been enemies either, never at conflict, but despite our similarities, we've never really been at ease when left in each other's company. We both love music, like the same kinds of food; we each have a hard-wired habit of saying the incalculably wrong thing in any given situation and an inclination towards queasiness while drinking ale. These things should unite us, but put us in a room together and we adopt the stilted conversational style of two strangers forced into each other's orbit at a party.

'Have you two met?' the host might say. 'I'm sure you'll get on. You have so much in common.'

While I would have self-immolated to get my mother's attention, I was always happy to leave my father to his own devices. To let him sit undisturbed, watching sport on TV or indulging in fastidious DIY projects. When I failed to be dynamic and sporty, he was disappointed. Then my brother Ben showed an interest in football and tennis and I felt relieved of the burden. I could indulge in my own pastimes, freed from my father's spotlight and scrutiny and time. With Ben soaking up his attention I was able to do whatever I wanted, without him being involved or judging me. And then I, we, had those forty months. Thirty-nine. Counting down. With his heart, maybe thirty? Add in the kidney disease and what, twenty-five?

So, when my mother and sister booked a burlesque tour of Tenerife in September of 2019 and my father needed someone to take him to see his cancer specialist, I volunteered myself immediately. I booked some time off work and drove over to Withernsea, dedicating myself to the idea of compressing forty-three years of distance into two days. When I learned that my little brother Ben wanted to come along too, I saw an even better opportunity. The three remaining Farrer men, together under the same roof for the first time in what must have been twenty-five years. We would hang out, drink, talk, laugh together. Bond. All of the things we never did because we'd always been reluctant or incapable.

Time still had a hold on us back then and the five hours in the waiting room of the hospital in Hull felt almost injurious. My father stared into space, I sat reading a Patti Smith memoir and Ben fiddled with his phone, Googling miracle super-foods and supplements that might stall or reverse our father's cancer while Macmillan volunteers plied us with biscuits and hot drinks. The three of us, united as we'd never been and as uncomfortable together as we'd always been, waiting to find out when one of us would die.

'Spirulina,' Ben said, leaning over to our father. 'And Golden Milk.'

'Sorry?' my father replied, confused by what he considered to be demented non-sequiturs.

'They'll give you more ...' Ben paused then, wanting to say, 'time, they'll give you more time with us' but searching for a word that didn't suggest some kind of end point. 'They're healthy. They'll keep you healthy.'

'Oh, right,' our father said distantly, distracted by the offer of a biscuit from one of the volunteers. 'That's good.'

Ben and I were under orders from our mother to pay atten-tion to everything the doctor said at the appointment, to ask questions. My father, defiant in his deafness and refusing to succumb to a hearing aid, will often reply in the affirmative or nod in understanding even if the thing that is being said sounds to him as if it's being indistinctly whispered through a keyhole. In recent years our conversations have taken on the shape of a confusing improv routine.

'They're talking about redundancies at work again,' I might say.

'Yes, I feel the same way.' He'll reply, hedging his bets with a positive response.

'If it happens to me, I could lose the house.'

'Yes, alright then. Good idea.'

Frustrated by this sort of thing, I would often make a game of it, seeing what I could get away with saying. I might make him a cup of tea, then add with a smile 'Do you want me to spit in that?'

'Yes, thank you,' he'd reply. 'That'd be lovely.'

'I've made it with water from the toilet,' I'd say, handing a mug to him.

He'd gratefully take it from me then, cupping it in both hands and taking a small, satisfying sip.

'Lovely.'

But these kinds of games lost their fun once I learned that he was dying. So, I did my duty and paid attention when we finally reached the consultation room, Ben and I quizzing the doctor about every detail. Trying to squeeze a promise of more time out of him. The meeting was quick and the news was largely positive. We learned that the cancer was not yet at a stage where it required chemo or some other drastic measures. That the protein levels in his blood hadn't changed.

'So, as long as those levels don't change,' Ben asked, 'then he can keep going and going, right?'

'In theory,' the doctor said, turning from his screen of figures to face us. 'But nothing is certain.'

'Yeah, yeah, but that's good isn't it?'

'Yes,' the doctor said, allowing himself a smile. 'That's good.'

But later, when we WhatsApped our mother to report the news, she was confused, Ben and I each interpreting the information differently. From me she learned that the situation hadn't worsened. From Ben she learned that as long as the myeloma continues to stall our father is potentially immortal. In the immediate aftermath though, we were all celebratory. I took the two of them to a fish and chip restaurant on the way home and we all ordered big, wolfing our food and savouring it because it seemed that we finally all had licence to enjoy the pleasure of our senses. Confident then, I suggested my plan, that all three of us should hang out together that evening and continue the celebrations. Ben had other ideas though and asked that I drop him off at a friend's house on the way back to Withernsea, as he wanted to watch the football instead. I said that was fine, figuring that I at least had my father and time and hope. When we got back home and my father was happily settled down on the sofa, I offered to get us some wine.

'I can't drink,' he said. 'It interferes with my heart medication.'

'Shall we watch a film then?' I said, switching on the TV and selecting the movie channel, where the opening scenes of a film starring Lady Gaga were playing.

'Oh,' he said. 'This is the one where she becomes a big success, and he dies at the end isn't it?'

'Apparently,' I said.

'Shall we watch that *Winnie the Pooh* film instead?'

'Does *he* die in the end?'

'Oh, everyone dies in the end.'

# Cold Fish Soup

We sat there for a while, feeling no further need to talk, until a friend texted me to ask how things were going. I told her honestly and she replied with a poem called 'Bookends' by Tony Harrison, about a non-communicative father and son, separated from each other by their persistent and dominant silence. She said that, no offence, but it reminded her of my father and me. I read it on my phone while the two of us sat at opposite ends of the sofa, allowing the blare of the TV to fill the silence that always existed between us whenever my mother wasn't in the room.

That my father and I don't really talk to each other doesn't matter that much when she is around, always there to flood the space between us with her anecdotes and tall tales. One of her talents is that she can recall great reams of dialogue without stumbling and is fond of reciting 'Jabberwocky' in its entirety. Not a hugely long poem, I guess, but a strangely mangled one that she often breaks into without warning. Sometimes just to amuse herself and other times to lift a glum atmosphere in a room. And I think it's because of this that, whenever I read poems, I think of her voice. The way she possesses the words. This meant that, although she was absent, reading 'Bookends' made her present. The words seeming like her commentary on my relationship with my father, a banging together of our heads.

*You're like book ends, the pair of you ...*
*... say nothing, sit, sleep, stare ...*

I felt this poem. Registered the sad notion that only our silence made my father and me a pair, then did nothing to act upon it. Mostly because, by the time I'd finished reading my father was asleep and snoring, but also because I wouldn't have said anything anyway. Neither of us would ever do anything so blatantly affectionate as express love for one another, but we each implicitly know that it's a given and that saying it out loud would only ruin the pleasant, reassuring feeling that we got from knowing we'd never have to. So, I watched him sleep, his mouth lolling open and his breathing growing heavier, while over on the TV a terrified Pooh shuddered at the notion of the Heffalump.

My father had perhaps been asleep in this way for half an hour when he suddenly woke with a small yell and a look of panic on his face, as if startled by something explosive and, in the process, startling me too. My reflex was to immediately consider a medical complaint. Was it his heart? Can a kidney burst?

'Do you want some stewed apple?' he said, turning to me then briskly pushing himself to his feet and heading into the kitchen. 'Your mum made some before she went away.'

Without waiting for me to answer he came back and handed me a bowl of stewed apple and custard, the contents slopped over the rim. Then the two of us sat in silence again, eating at opposite ends of the room. Each of us like fucking bookends, wasting time while the months ticked away. Twenty-four. Twenty-three. Twenty-two …

\*

When lockdown started I wasn't too concerned about my family. It was a time of no visiting. No hugs. Of regular phone calls and long-distance tenderness. For most people it would be a struggle, but I thought of it as something I'd been in training for, geographic necessity already stretching our bond and our love across the Pennines. This distance though, had always been a choice. I knew that I could visit whenever I liked. But now, with the pandemic, the thread that connected us felt strained and uncomfortable, frayed. I heard horror stories of deaths and of families not being allowed to attend funerals. I thought of my father dying alone in a room, gagging on a ventilator. I worried I might not get back to the town to see my father before it was too late. And less so, to finish this book that had started out as a collection of stories about a place and had turned into a distraction from my death, and a record of other peoples.

Trapped at home, I lived online and grabbed hope where I could get it. On Twitter I watched a *BBC Look North* piece on Dean Wilson, interviewed on his phone while standing on Withernsea beach, discussing his pebble walks.

'I've been writing more than I ever wrote before,' he said, his hood up, the rain lashing him. 'On the beach I feel comforted. On the beach, I don't know what loneliness is ...'

In the @ replies someone had responded with 'Ah, there's the life I've been looking for' and it was a strange feeling, to see somewhere I had lived being pined for and idealised in this way. They wanted Dean's life. My life. And it was cut off from me. This shithole. My shithole. And I missed it.

As soon as I was cleared to travel, I drove over to Withernsea to see my family. My sister, Becky, my brother-in-law, my mum and dad, all congregated in my parent's garden, each of us carrying folding chairs and moving cautiously, as if traversing a minefield. We positioned ourselves at two-metre intervals and sat down with mugs, a stone circle of anxious tea drinkers. There was something tense in the air and we were all aware of what it was; that one wrong move, one stray breath, and we could kill our father. He seemed pretty content though, and largely fearless. His life hadn't changed, instead the world had adjusted around him.

# There Is a Light That Never Goes Out

When he headed into the house to feed the pets I saw a chance and took a photo of him from the doorway, wanting to preserve every normal moment that I could before weight loss and hospital beds took over. In the image he is standing there by the worktop, surrounded by his cats and dogs, who are all looking up at him and tracking his movements like flowers following the sun. I was keen to capture him going about his daily business but as he placed the bowls on the kitchen floor he looked up and caught me taking another photo, becoming immediately self-conscious.

'What do you want?' he asked, his cheeks colouring.

'For you to go and live in the nuclear bunker and wait until all this is over.'

This was the first thing that popped into my head when he asked me. On the outskirts of town, not far from my parents' house, there is a decommissioned cold war-era nuclear bunker. It's now a tourist attraction and people often get married there, but crucially it sits 100 feet underground and has a blast door. There is no safer place for miles around.

'But I don't want to live in a bunker.'

'I don't want you to die.'

'Well, I'm not that keen myself,' he said, reaching into the back of the cupboard for a packet of chocolate biscuits.

*

Once we'd spent a while in the garden I took Millie for a walk into the town to see how it was looking after a few months in lockdown. I'd been dependent on updates about it from family members who weren't leaving the house very often and could only speculate on how things were going. We wandered down the atrophied high street, where every closed and shuttered storefront looked dead and brittle somehow, as if, had I reached out to touch one, it would have crinkled and flaked like dry leaves. But I didn't, because no one touched anything anymore. When we reached the locked-up Army recruitment building we crossed the road and looped back around, heading past the shuttered arcades. Outside Smiles for Miles a few people in masks were selling handicrafts from pasting tables, but I didn't stop to browse, not wanting to carry home anything dangerous and infect my father. Instead, we headed over to the valley gardens, where a young man stood alone bouncing a tennis ball against a wall, a shell-suited Steve McQueen waiting for, if not a great escape, then at least for the arcades to open again, so he could restart his life and get back to beating his high score on Dance Dance Revolution. Behind him, towering over everything, stood the lighthouse, a small light visible at the top. Hardly the seeking beam the news story had suggested. Not so much a beacon of hope as a glimmer, but there nonetheless.

Millie and I walked back to my parent's house and we all said our goodbyes on their doorstep. At the moment when we would all traditionally hug and kiss, we faltered, unsure of how to approach it when we weren't allowed to touch. For want of anything better, Becky hugged herself tightly, swaying gently, as she does when she holds me. The rest of us followed suit, metres apart, swaying, self-hugging. All bar my dad, who only really has it in him to hug pets and mint condition vinyl albums. So, he watched, uncomfortable, as we did this awkward dance on his driveway.

'Drive safely,' he said, and somehow this seemed to be a little too much emotion for him to be showing, so he headed back into the house. My mother remained by the front door as I got in the car and drove off, watching her in the rear-view mirror. Still self-hugging, swaying, shrinking.

*

Later, on the motorway, I called Zoe on speaker and she asked me how my day had gone.

'Fine,' I said. 'It was all good. Everyone's okay.'

I didn't tell her that I was scared for my father. That while I didn't believe in angels, I'd still hedged my bets and asked them three times to spare him anyway. Not asking that he be allowed to live forever, just that he outlive the beacon of hope and that I didn't have to see many more of his months ticking away from a distance. Twenty-one. Twenty. Nineteen …

'But never mind that,' I said, 'how are you doing?'

'God,' she said, breathing heavily. 'Where do I start?'

'At the beginning,' I said, 'don't spare the details.'

I kept my mouth shut then and listened to her talk about a problem with work, enjoying the sound of her voice, the twists and tangents she took, and the escape of a story that wasn't about me.

# The Museum of Withernsea

My dog, Millie, sits most of the time these days, because she cannot stand for long. If we spend too much time in one spot her back legs will gradually give way like a punctured inflatable, lowering her to the ground. So, on walks we either keep moving or we give in to the collapse. When we stop, she often chooses my feet to rest on, because they're big and I don't move anywhere fast. Waiting outside Ellis's Cafe, just off Withernsea promenade, her choice was either my trainers or the concrete, so she lumped down onto my feet and shimmied up to me, resting her head against my knees.

I adopted her back in September of 2019 when she'd just turned fifteen and was by far the most unwanted dog in the kennels. I'd already decided to pick the oldest one they had, but Millie was something else. A twice abandoned Labrador, too sick and old to live up to anyone's dream of what a family dog should be. In truth she's a Labrador cross, though crossed with what no one is sure. Whatever it was, she's ended up looking like a failed but still remarkable experiment. A first draft you just want to leave unchanged. She's barrel-shaped with stumpy legs and pig-pink skin, visible through an off-white coat that moults away from her in downy, fist-sized tumble weeds whenever she sneezes, which is roughly every five minutes.

When one of the handlers brought her out of the kennels and over to me for the first time, Millie was on the brink of collapse, awkwardly sashaying like a catwalk model attempting to navigate a runway in precarious heels. Her tongue hung from one side of her mouth like a half-eaten rasher of thick-cut bacon, making her look appealingly dopey and lost in thought. She was deaf, had diarrhoea and her shaggy body was studded with egg-sized tumours. Twice daily medication was required to help ease the pain from the arthritis in her hips. The front part of her body was okay, home to healthy organs and a pair of front legs that a powerlifter would be proud of, but her hind legs were so withered at that point they looked as if they'd been plucked from a chicken on its death bed. Still, possessed by a youthful energy that her body couldn't quite sustain, the realisation that she was being taken for a walk overtook her and she attempted to bound towards me, at which point she lost her balance and tumbled headfirst into a hedge. I fell in love with her immediately.

The handler, a stout middle-aged woman named Jane, placed Millie's lead in my hand.

'Take her for a spin,' Jane said, smiling. 'But not too fast.'

A four-legged tragedy, tectonic plates moved faster than Millie. On top of the arthritis, she also had an inner ear infection that was affecting her balance, so she had to be held upright with her harness in order to stop her from falling over. This made walking her an act closer to puppeteering. As we picked our way around the grounds she turned all corners with trepidation, approaching each as if it was both her first time doing so, but also as if it could be her last.

'Is it fair to keep her alive?' I asked Jane, as I crouched to stroke Millie's ears and stare lovingly into her drooping, mournful eyes.

'Well, the vets say she's okay,' Jane said, 'but she'll be lucky if she makes it past Christmas.' I must have done something drastic with my face because she looked flustered and quickly recalibrated, switching to the positive. 'She's happy and playful though. Plenty of miles left in her.'

It was weird to be offered a dog by someone who kept using car sales talk. Like getting the hard sell on a cut-and-shut: two cars that have clearly been welded together. And in fairness, that was Millie – a canine cut-and-shut. Front end decent, back end bad. But, me being a sucker for a lost cause and a short-term let with character, I adopted Millie that day. Jane and I sat in the reception area, going through the paperwork, while Millie tottered around the room like a cartoon drunk, eventually collapsing at my feet and looking up at me with so much unwarranted adoration that I felt woozy from it. I fussed her ears as I read through her notes, pausing when I reached the section on personality quirks.

'It says here that she's a bit of a diva.'

'Oh yeah,' Jane replied, her eyes widening, 'she's a diva alright.'

I looked at Millie lying on the floor, barely capable of breathing, let alone outrageous demands. She struggled to her feet and briskly farted from the exertion.

'Are you going to change her name?' Jane asked, as I signed the adoption papers.

'Yes,' I said, watching as Millie slowly navigated a doorway and collided with the frame. 'I'm going to call her Lightning. Or Mariah Carey.'

'Really?'

'No,' I said. 'Why change the name of a deaf dog?'

'That's all the more reason,' Jane said. 'You can call her anything you like. What she doesn't know won't hurt her.'

The kennels usually charged £150 for adoptions but they didn't think it was right to charge me that kind of money just so I could watch a dog die. It wasn't that kind of business.

'Maybe just make a donation,' Jane said. 'How does £20 sound?'

'Are you sure?'

'Yeah,' she said. 'It seems fair.'

I settled up and walked Millie to the car, my third-hand, £20 puppet, and hoisted her up into the back seat. *I love you*, I thought. And something else. *I've saved you.*

\*

Outside Ellis's cafe, Millie shifted her position on my feet and looked up at me, squinting from the late-summer sun. Almost sixteen now and well past the Christmas she was never expected to reach, her eyes resemble crystal balls, milky with cataracts. She can still see light and shapes though. On the days when she's stable enough to be let off her lead she easily loses sight of me, panics and follows the blurry outlines of passers-by in the hope that they're me. When I catch up with her, she realises her error and turns back to me with the slow, laboured movement of a freighter changing course. To avoid her stress and struggle, I tend to keep her safe and close.

'Good girl,' I told her, stroking her ears, these defunct flaps of velveteen cloth. I'd heard that deaf dogs don't realise they're deaf, they just think you're ignoring them, so I like to get up close and put in the effort, looking her in the eyes. 'She won't be long.'

We were waiting for my new girlfriend, Emma, who had headed inside to pick us up some sandwiches. We'd known each other for a while but had only really started talking just before the first COVID-19 lockdown. We had struck upon the idea of taking trips to the kinds of resort towns that other people might have baulked at – our mission to find joy in maligned, off-season coastal places. Fleetwood, Rhyl, anywhere we stood a reasonable chance of getting struck by lightning while exiting a bingo hall. The first place we chose was Morecambe, defying an amber storm warning and driving through sheets of dense rain and skidding motorway traffic, determined to get in our idea of fun no matter what the obstacle was. Halfway there, squinting through my windscreen, I grew concerned that I was going to crash the car and kill the both of us. That this was how I would die, and horribly. Not with a decision on a cliff edge or with any sense of my own agency but with the panicked jerk of a wheel. A blurted swear. I wouldn't have been the first person whose final words were 'Oh shit!' and I wouldn't have been the last, but it seemed typical. That my stupidity would cause me to hurtle off a motorway bridge and to my doom, at a time when death had begun to lose its allure, taking someone else with me in the process. As we approached the coastline though, the slate sky gave way to something blue and pure. We were probably on the fringe of the storm, maybe at the eye of it and still at risk, but it felt curiously safe. We quickly forgot the danger and instead strolled the promenade, ate chips and cake, visited the arcades and won a small polystyrene plane on the penny falls, which we took to the beach, threw into the air and never saw again. The storm had picked up by that point, so we took a walk to the end of the stone jetty that thrusts out into Morecambe Bay, leaning into the wind as we fought our way towards a bench bolted to the end of it. Here we sat, 250 metres out to sea, staring at the storm and eating jelly sweets. Waves crashing at the sides of the jetty and spitting up at us.

'This is how a lighthouse must feel,' I said, thinking of one that wasn't Withernsea's.

'Cold and lonely?' Emma asked.

'Not lonely,' I replied, 'just cold. And exposed.' In truth I didn't feel that cold either. Her knee was touching my thigh, warming it. Increasing my heart rate and setting off my internal heating system. 'Let's stay here a bit longer.'

When the fierce wind began to rob us of the sense of feeling in our faces and our hair became matted with sea spray, we decided it was time to leave, fighting our way down the jetty and back to the car. Then we drove back through the storm, talking as we avoided roads closed by flooding, rain lashing at the windscreen, and after I'd dropped her home, I felt a strong sense of having left something important behind.

A few days later, the COVID-19 pandemic forced everyone into their homes and we were cut off from one another. So, we charted our courtship through lockdown and the socially distanced months that would follow, sending timid texts at first that gradually progressed into essay-length missives. Conducted pining bedtime chats over WhatsApp video until we burned out on words and fell asleep. As we approached the autumn of 2020, we had become so revoltingly into one another that, had this relationship fully played out in the physical world, one of us would have surely swallowed the other whole. As it was, kisses were at first limited to emojis. Words and feelings were lost in the digital decay and screen freeze. Others were amplified, our happy faces frozen as the broadband infrastructure strained to cope with a nation of people doing the same thing. Peering through the pixels.

'Are you still there?'

'Yes, I'm still here. You froze.'

'You froze too.'

'I love you.'

'Sorry, what was that? You froze again.'

'I said I love you.'

'I know, I lied. I just wanted to hear you say it again.'

It felt like we were living through a glitch in reality. Crumbling somehow, both of us losing our sense of who we were. It was scary and intangible, so to hold ourselves together, to hold on to each other, we talked around those feelings, discussing the places we'd go when it was all over and the world had reassembled. We talked of the places and things we wanted to show each other, all the countries we'd visit. But first, I wanted to take Emma to Withernsea. I'd tell her about it often, pushing its shabby charm, detailing all the ways in which it was and had been mine. I built it up into a crown of flawed gems and paste diamonds. In terms of maligned coastal towns, it was my holy land, and I was impatient to show her all of it. If she went there and liked it, saw in it what I did, then I felt certain the relationship we were building would be the real thing. Love me, love Withernsea. It was a big ask.

More than anywhere else that Emma and I had planned on visiting together, Withernsea had a life expectancy. It was both going somewhere and nowhere, dissolving like sugar into the tea-coloured sea. Throughout the pandemic, I'd been tuned to consider disaster and was quietly thinking about what will be left one day when Withernsea, like all of the lost towns and villages before it, is gone and largely forgotten. Perhaps because so few people seemed to care, and because I was trapped in my house with nothing but time on my hands, I'd started making a list of the ways that I would preserve the memory of the town. A list that I could present to Emma. It wouldn't necessarily be everyone's Withernsea, but my own personal version, capturing all the things about the town that were important to me before it disappeared. Lost to the sea or financial ruin. So, I imagined a space; a vast, warehouse-sized exhibition hall and gallery that I could curate, filling it with the things that represented the town's value to me. The Museum of Withernsea.

I don't know what I thought I was doing really, but if nothing else it was a way of occupying my mind when so many people around me seemed to be losing theirs to boredom, fear and anxiety. I was still working on my book, but I also had more time trapped with my thoughts than I knew what to do with, so when I wasn't writing my manuscript, I wrote to release the pressure in my head, filling the museum and gallery walls with these extra words. I guessed it was the sort of thing that people did in prison. Locked up, they focus on all the things that are important to them and everything they'll see and do when they get out. Locked down, I did the same. I thought of the things I would drag inland, if money, imagination and technology were no barrier, then stuff into The Museum of Withernsea. The sooner Emma saw the town the way I did, I thought, the sooner I could feel secure that it was all going to work out.

The idea of the museum bounced around in my head until it was vigorous enough to start waking me in the night. Each time it did, I would pull out a notebook and add to my list of ideas for exhibits, writing expanded description cards for each, little essays I suppose. Once written, my brain purged, I would fall back to sleep. Looking through my notes in the morning, I'd find that some of these ideas were rational and uncomplicated, while others looked like the follies of an obsessed and eccentric billionaire.

EXHIBIT 1: A large piece of granite rock wall displayed alongside a single Dean Wilson pebble.

EXHIBIT 2: Transcript of a text message sent to Mark Vernon, never responded to, asking for a progress report on his investigation. Words will be etched onto the chest of a seven-foot waxwork werewolf.

EXHIBIT 3: Replica of teenage bedroom. Installation/daily performance piece by actor in costume, miming to Run-D.M.C and Aerosmith's 'Walk This Way'.

EXHIBIT 4: Olympic-sized saltwater wave pool, with fudge-coloured beach feature.

EXHIBIT 5: Daily musical performance of song written after Robert's funeral, titled 'Second-hand Hallelujah' and played from a coffin-shaped music box.

EXHIBIT 6: Union Jack nipple tassels mounted on a spot-lit, doric-style plinth in front of a wall-sized projection of Ruby Reds performances, set on a constant loop.

EXHIBIT 7: Robert's Flowerbed. Container filled with soil and positioned in a white, open space.

EXHIBIT 8: Scale model of a Golden Sands chalet, poised on the lip of a fifteen-foot mocked-up cliff made from Withernsea clay and engineered to erode, causing the chalet to fall and shatter. Exhibit rebuilt for the first of each month, when the process repeats.

On its way to nowhere anyone wanted to go, my museum was a place you might pop your head through the door of if you somehow happened to be passing through, but you never would be. And that was fine, Withernsea is not for everyone and by association, neither would its museum be. While some exhibits might seem frivolous, others were vital and permanent. Sacred.

*

## Exhibit 7

The flowerbed where Robert's body was discovered was nothing if not unspectacular. One of those black, charmless containers made of some kind of dense, vulcanised plastic and branded with the logo of the local council. In a million years it will likely look exactly the same, divorced from all meaning or purpose. You'd never know it was once home to civic blooms or acted as the final resting place of a thirty-seven-year-old father of six. It has long ago been removed from the promenade, but it was there for about a year after Robert died. On trips back to the town I would make a point of visiting it, either driving by to give it a respectful nod or to stop and touch it, in the same way I had after his funeral.

On that day, the wake at his house had been too much for me. His widow, Clare, barely holding it together, his children too young for the most part to comprehend that he wasn't going to turn up at some point and join the party. Those family members who understood that Robert was never coming back huddled together in his living room, sipping spirits from tea-cups and sharing stories about him. Good ones. Treasured ones. Teary-eyed remember when's. None of the difficult tales that had led us to that day. The few bad memories that were spoken of were repurposed as light-hearted anecdotes. The time he fell off his roof while drunk was recounted like a scene from an old comedy show. Our family's equivalent of Del Boy falling through the bar.

At one point we all headed into the garden and gathered to write messages to Robert, tie them to helium-filled balloons and release them into the sky. I wrote 'You idiot. I love you' then batted my balloon into the air, never believing that it would reach Robert but amused by the idea that it might land in the path of a moron who needed to feel wanted. The stupidity of this thought got me giggling and once I started, I found that I couldn't stop. Of all people it was my father who picked up on this as a sign that I wasn't dealing with things very well, so he offered to take me to the place where Robert's body was found. On paper, this is the worst thing that anyone could have asked, but he knew that it was exactly what I needed.

My father and I walked down to the seafront and stopped a few feet away from the flower bed, which rested against the wall that faced the pier entrance. The flowers, along with the body, removed.

'He was there,' my father said, pointing to the bed, then he stepped away and turned to look out to sea. I don't know if he just felt uncomfortable or if he was granting me time and room to think, but the result was the same. Not really knowing how to react, I tried to think of the ways I'd seen grieving people behaving in movies. A scene that would be captured with mournful strings. So, I reached out to the bed and let the soil glance the tips of my fingers. Wanting to make contact with the last place Robert's living body had touched. It was a start. Quite Hallmark movie of me but okay. I'd meant it though, and that was what was important. I tried then to think of something significant to say, to who or what I wasn't sure, but instead found myself thinking of something Robert had once told me about death.

'When you die your body completely relaxes and all the piss and shit drains out of it,' he said. His face had lit up with pleasure as he watched mine crumple in disgust, so he kept going. 'All of it, even the stuff that's been inside you for years, rotting. It all slips out.'

I withdrew my hand and stood in front of the flowerbed, thinking about what I might have just put my fingers in and of how much he'd have liked to have seen that. How much he'd have laughed at the sight of it and how alive he looked when he did.

'Bits of a Mars bar you ate when you were five, all that comes out of you too. Like soup. Splootch.'

## *Exhibit 3*

In news that stunned all of us, my parents managed to sell their home near the cliffs. A cash buyer looking for a bargain put in an offer just before the pandemic hit. I was told that the new owners had no heirs and seemed to be pretty certain that they wouldn't live to see their flowerbeds being lapped at by the North Sea. My parents kept their mouths shut, took the money and moved further inland, to a smaller place. A dormer bungalow next to Withernsea golf course. My father used some of the money they'd made to buy himself a red Audi A3 that sits on their new drive, largely untouched but making him happy all the same. The bungalow is their home, not mine, and I feel kind of strange when I call it 'home', because it's not. Our house by the cliffs was. The mural of Joe Perry on my bedroom wall had long been papered over by my father, but I knew it was always there and within reach, my parents its passive custodians. Now someone else had taken on that role. A stranger, who may one day discover it and wonder about the kind of person who'd once lived within those walls. I did a lot in that room. Read. Played my bass. Wrote my manifestos and thought about girls. But when I picture myself in that space, what I am doing is a forward flip.

I am not a physically gifted person. In PE classes I only seemed to do okay in lighter activities like badminton or volleyball. Sports that required me to keep my distance from the other players and where the objective was not to possess a projectile but to get rid of it. If the rules amounted to 'Keep that thing away from me, I don't want it!' then it was an activity I could get behind. When my school briefly trialled non-competitive sports I was relieved to be given the opportunity to reject cricket in favour of improvised dance. I spent a pleasant few weeks flinging my limbs around to hits of the '70s and '80s, but when my school realised that it was unlikely to win trophies for my interpretations of 'Thriller' and 'Car Wash', it quietly dropped the programme and began to focus on rugby, a sport that suited me like your grandpa suits hotpants. I pledged to never throw myself into a sport again. But watching Steven Tyler doing a handspring front flip in the music video for 'Walk This Way', I somehow struck upon the notion that I was capable of doing it myself.

I was midway through my Tyler phase at that point. Tight jeans, a turquoise shirt knot-tied at my waist and one of my mother's shimmering, silky scarves tied around my wrist. I'm not sure if believing I looked the part led me to understand that I was ready, without practice or preparation, to do this. But while I had not executed so much as a forward roll since primary school, I cleared a space at the foot of my bed and mentally calculated the distance I had to work with. Steven Tyler seemed to be able to manage this move in an area of about three square feet. We're about the same height and I'd given myself about six feet so, feeling ready, I took a breath, put my hands out in front of me and launched myself forward.

You get more thinking time when hurling through the air than you'd expect. Too much, in fact. Enough to allow you to fully comprehend your situation and potential fate. I knew that things were not going my way from the moment my hands hit the ground, aware of everything my body was doing. The way my wrists were struggling to bear my weight, causing me to go off centre. How my body was twisting backwards before my legs had even travelled over my head. And finally, of the sickly crack and thud as I collapsed like a detonated tower block and landed on my head, the middle of my spine colliding with the corner of my black ash desk.

'What was that?' my father yelled up the stairs.

'Nothing!' I gasped, while I lay on the floor, scared to move. Wondering if any further motion might paralyse me.

'It didn't sound like nothing!'

I wiggled my fingers, my toes. Gingerly rolled onto my side.

'Do you want me to come up?' my father said.

'NO!' I shouted, because how would I explain myself? Lying on the floor, dressed like a peacock. Having to say 'Well, you know that bit in the "Walk This Way" video …' An explanation didn't bear thinking about. My back still hurt though. Badly. I put my hand on the source of the pain and felt a wetness. I brought my hand to my face and saw that a sizeable amount of blood was leaking from a wound. I wondered if you could see my spine through it, so I pushed myself to my feet and headed to the bathroom to check in the mirror. Looking over my shoulder at the reflection of my back, I saw a three-inch gouge running down the centre of my spine, as if I'd been hooked and dragged. I then caught the reflection of my face. Pale, sick with worry and, as usual, not in the least like Steven Tyler.

While memories fade and buildings drop from sight in billowing clouds of brick dust, scars remain. I fully expect mine to outlast my home on the cliffs.

## Exhibit 5

Before I could bring myself to write stories about Robert, I wrote a song about him. It was pretty simple, in A major, and somewhere between Led Zeppelin's 'Thank You' and a maudlin Mark Lanegan country ballad. No one has heard it but me because I only wrote it for Robert. A direct reaction to his funeral at a crematorium in Hull.

Though it was April, it had snowed heavily in the days leading up to the service and a thick, frozen layer gripped the grounds. Before the funeral began, I'd quickly reached my limit for well-meaning platitudes and stepped outside to get some air then promptly threw up behind the crematorium. After I'd finished retching, I looked up to see a man in the memorial gardens staring at me in silence. In one hand he held a bunch of geraniums, with the other he worried at an itch beside his groin. I felt exposed and ashamed, so immediately headed back inside to the toilets, where I rinsed my mouth at the sink then took my seat in the pews between Becky and Ben. I looked over at Robert's coffin, resting on an elevated plinth behind the lectern. The presence and absence of him was crushing, an emotional and physical pressure. I wanted to throw up again.

As the service progressed, thoughts of the living Robert overtook my nausea. It struck me that his funeral was something that he would have laughed at and wanted to disrupt. I considered the ways that he'd have found to do that. His urge to be inappropriate in the most serious of situations, always directing his mid-portions at authority. The structure of the service was broadly Anglican, the proceedings led by a priest who wore her hair like Jon Bon Jovi in the video for 'Bad Medicine' and spoke in the kind of dull, sticky tones I'm now familiar with from ASMR videos. She'd never met Robert but had been provided with some mundane details of his life, which she talked about as if he had been proud of them. Low points, really. His job as a warehouse stock checker. His dwindling interest in motorcycles. She'd made him sound boring, staid and sedate, which could never be said of him. If she'd wanted to capture the real Robert she would have spoken of his curious compulsion towards the things that were bad for him or the joy he got from holding people down, lowering his trousers and farting directly into their ears. One thing she did get right though, was the music; in place of the hymns, were the songs of Ozzy Osbourne.

'Robert loved life,' the priest said, finishing off one of her wispy platitudes. 'Now please be silent for "Paranoid" by Black Sabbath.'

There we were, a building full of sobbing loved ones, sideswiped by grief, our heads bowed in solemn contemplation while Tony Iommi ripped a blazing solo and Ozzy sang of his tormented mental state. This was followed by 'Changes', 'No More Tears' and, with a lack of awareness that made me feel light-headed, 'Crazy Train'. When that spiralling riff started up there was a moment when I felt certain Robert was about to leap out of the coffin and, laughing himself hoarse, reveal that we'd all been pranked in the darkest ever episode of MTV's *Punk'd*.

Along with the humour though, there was rage. I don't know who else felt it, but I did. An anger that we all had to go through this. That we had to watch his two sons, too young to comprehend the situation and all the crying, walking up to mourners and handing out tissues. While I knew this was bigger than one simple intervention, I wished Robert could have carried on walking until he'd reached my parents' house, or my sister's, but instead he ended up in a flowerbed and we all ended up in a crematorium.

I left the service feeling winded and lost but as the days went on, the exceptional madness of the service stuck with me beyond the way a normal funeral would have. So, I began writing a song about it. About how we had celebrated him using a faith he found ridiculous, then somehow made things more so. The title came first, 'Second-hand Hallelujah'. I wasn't sure it made sense, but it had a nice ring to it and, ready to carry on in that poetic vein, I sat down to work on the lyrics, expecting florid words to leak from my pen as if gripped by the spirit of Byron. I was forgetting two things: that I didn't understand poetry and that, when faced with emotions, my response is to do everything I could to avoid them.

Writing heartfelt lyrics has always made me feel queasy and, as hard as I tried, I could never throw myself into them without cringing. Writing a song about Robert had been no different. I tried tweaking the music, adding subtle chord changes and trills, languid rhythms, trying to encourage some elegant words out of myself, but still they clunked out of me as childish limericks. In truth these were the sorts of things that Robert loved to sing. Songs that began with 'There was a young lady from Ealing,' and ended with a description of an act so disgraceful it would require a three-person crew to clean up. And really, I had to think of my audience; not one that wanted artful poetry, but a dead guy who liked dick jokes. So, I thought about what had happened on the day of his funeral, of how I'd felt, and wrote about that, in a style designed to appeal to Robert alone. No one else needed to like it.

# Cold Fish Soup

*There was no air to breathe*
*And I could not accept this*
*So, I took to the grounds*
*Where I threw up my breakfast*
*The snow on the grass*
*Now looked like a Pollock*
*And a guy holding flowers*
*Watched while scratching his bollocks*
*It's a mess*
*And you made it*
*You should have come home ...*
*No laughter, no farts*
*Not the you in our hearts*
*Just a view of a box*
*Full of dead body parts*
*And if you were up there*
*If you could have seen us*
*You'd have come down from wherever*
*And shown us your penis*
*It's a mess*
*And you made it*
*You should have come home ...*
*I considered my pain*
*The thoughts that would linger*
*Of how you'd never again*
*Ask me 'please pull my finger'*
*Try as I might*
*It didn't feel like the right thing*
*I could not make it work*
*It just sounded like typing*
*Still, I wrote you this song*

*But I won't write another*
*'Cause the words came out wrong*
*Just like you and me, brother*
*It's a mess*
*And you made it*
*You should have come home ...*

I've not sung this song in years, but there is a recording of it, free with all purchases from the museum gift shop. It will only play once and deletes itself immediately afterwards. It cannot be returned and has no monetary value.

*

Working on my list of exhibits in the night, I'd often get interrupted by the clatter of Millie's feet on the floor downstairs. A clicking, scuffing tap dance, meaning that she was off the sofa and I had just a few seconds to clamber out of bed and down the stairs to let her out into the yard. She is often surprised by her own body upon waking and if I don't reach her in time there's a good chance that she'll release a series of panicked turds onto the floor then start anxiously padding them back and forth through the house, a situation nobody wants.

While she has lived beyond all expectations, Millie in late 2020 looked like a reanimated cockentrice, with her piggy front portions and those increasingly mangled-looking chicken legs bringing up the rear. Her steps are more like shuffles now, four stiff legs swinging awkwardly. She moves like a clothes horse brought to life. But it's always after sleep that she is at her weakest, having spent hours lying on and deadening her arthritic limbs. Stretching out her front paws, she'll slither off the sofa and onto the floor, from where I must gather her up, set her on her feet and gently rub some feeling into her hind legs before sending her on her way. Often, when I let her out at night, she pauses at the open door, briefly uncertain before taking a small, readying shimmy and throwing herself out into the darkness, not knowing how or when she'll land. Her feet always seem to hit the ground sooner then she expects. Sometimes there is a stabilising wobble, others she lands like a pile of tossed firewood. But she always shakes it off, rights herself, then paces the yard, preparing to go through the discomfort of squatting. Once done she will stand in the dark, staring, unseeing, her head oscillating as she tries to get her bearings and identify a way back inside. I stand at the back door and activate the torch on my phone, looking out for the flinch of recognition as she spots the light and her route back inside. *Home.* She clatters towards the open door, as agile as a park bench, following then leaping towards the light.

Each month I take her for a check-up at the vets and they tell me the same thing. 'She's happy, a bit wobbly, but it's not time to let her go yet.' Millie is adept at this, stealing time. The short-term commitment I made, having told myself that my heart could take a brief love and loss, has been extended indefinitely. She charms every vet she meets with her irrepressibly snaky hips and a face that is now set to an expression of permanent and adorable confusion. They massage and extend her legs, feel along her spine then increase her meds and send her on her way, to stop and stare and piss in the ever-encroaching darkness.

Some days she is lively and can walk for hours. Others she lasts for ten minutes then throws herself to the ground, leaving me to scrape all twenty-eight kilograms of her up off the pavement and carry her home, appearing to onlookers like a man collecting roadkill. Millie plays up to this, head lolling, legs dangling, every inch the dead dog. When we reach my front door though, she rediscovers her energy and springs into the house then straight to the back yard, where she immediately squats to pee. She won't do it in public, always in her yard, where, aside from my concerned gaze, she has complete privacy. Then she'll hop back inside, sniff derisively at the contents of her food bowl and throw herself into her bed with a sigh and a huff of dismissive flatulence.

'Diva,' I say, my words unable to fall on deafer ears, though at times like this, if I found out her deafness was an act I wouldn't be at all surprised.

When she becomes both completely blind and deaf, when her hips no longer support her weight at all, when she can only piss while standing and food is no longer a reason to stagger to her feet, I've been told that this will be the time to let her go. Until then there is three a.m., me holding a torch at the back door, a sleepy, swaying lighthouse. My notebook waiting for me on my bedside table, filled with a barely legible scrawl.

\*

When lockdown eased in the summer of 2020 and I was able to see people again, I met with my friend Anna at the park and showed her my notebook, convinced that even half-finished, my museum idea was a brilliant one and was proud to share it.

'Jesus,' she said, looking up from my list of exhibits, 'has Emma seen this yet?'

'No, why?'

# Cold Fish Soup

'You want to show your new girlfriend a lump of rock and the place where your brother died, do you not see anything strange about that? It didn't strike you as weird or depressing? A little self-obsessed?'

'Well, it hadn't until now.'

'What's this?' she said, looking down at the list again. 'A song about your brother's funeral? And I don't even want to talk about your mum's tits on a pedestal. Look, I'm not being funny but maybe you need therapy.'

Anna is a trainee therapist, so this is always her suggestion. Not just for me, but for everyone. She's a therapy evangelical. Stub your toe and she'll try to track it back to your childhood. Every conversation we have seems like it could end with a bill and a follow-up appointment. This is because whenever we're together she has to actively stop herself from analysing me.

'I'm sorry,' she said, 'but y'know … it's obvious.'

'Why? Am I broken?'

'No, you're not broken. You just need … work. It's like when you adopted your dad.'

'Sorry?'

'When you adopted Millie. You couldn't be near your dad when he was ill and far away, so you adopted a sick, deaf, elderly dog so you could sit on the sofa with her instead.'

'Oh shit,' I said, thinking of all the nights when Millie and I had sat together at opposite ends of the sofa, watching Netflix original series in complete silence. 'Did I?'

'She's also a stand-in for Withernsea. You've adopted Withernsea.'

'Oh, come on,' I said, ready to push back at this. 'That's a bit too much. Can't it just be that I like old dogs?'

Anna tilted her head and fixed me with a look that existed in a point between pity and criticism. This is her superpower, and somewhere inside me a switch labelled *Self Awareness* flipped to the on position.

'Oh shit,' I said.

'Yep,' she said. 'Think about it. You went to those kennels and chose the saddest, most unwanted and close-to-death's-door dog they had, then you completely fell in love with it and now spend all your time worrying about its well-being. And what did you do when you moved to the saddest, most unwanted, close-to-death seaside town in Yorkshire?'

'Fell in love with it?'

'And?'

'And spent all my time worrying about it?'

'Exactly. It's not a bad thing. It's caring. You just like wrecks. And wrecks that remind you of other wrecks.'

I considered all those nights I'd spent losing myself to this strangely comforting idea of virtual exhibits. Of how, talking to Anna, Withernsea suddenly seemed like a town that was missing its idiot, and my growing suspicion was that this idiot was me.

'And you know,' Anna said, 'a seaside town can't love you back, but a dog can.'

'Okay,' I said. 'Stop fucking with me. I get it, you're very clever and I'm completely basic and readable.'

'I am, and you are. Also, I take it back. I do want to talk about your mum's tits on a pedestal.'

I brushed past this.

'So, I should ditch the museum idea?'

'Honestly, love, a ditch isn't deep enough. Push it into the sea.' She could see I was disappointed, so threw me a bone. 'Look,' she added gently, 'the book you're writing. That's the museum.'

# Cold Fish Soup

*

In late summer, when I finally managed to take Emma to Withernsea, what I managed to show her was its shuttered-up seafront. The dead high street. The locked doors of the lighthouse, closed until further notice. The light on but nobody home. And finally, Ellis's cafe, where several members of my family had once worked and where Emma now stood in a taped-off, socially distanced zone near the counter, waiting for veggie sausages to be griddled and laid onto soft, floury barms at a workstation once manned by Robert. When she finally appeared, smiling broadly, two bulging paper bags in her hand, Millie perked up, the scent of food hitting her system and reactivating her atrophied hips. We all headed over to the Valley Gardens to eat them, Millie stumbling at our feet, pining for scraps.

'I wish I could show you more of this place,' I said to Emma, easing a sausage from my sandwich and passing it into Millie's clapping mouth. 'It's not always like this.'

'Nowhere is always like this,' Emma replied. 'You don't have to apologise.'

'I suppose. I'm just impatient, I want to enjoy it with you.'

'It's okay,' she said. 'We have time. I'm not going anywhere.'

'I know,' I replied, and I believed that. Believed in her at least. That, somehow, she wasn't in a hurry to run and that I hadn't destroyed things by bringing her to this glum and troubled place.

When we finished our sandwiches, the three of us left the Valley Gardens and took a walk down to the beach. Millie lost her balance at first, slipping on the pebbles as if they'd been buttered, but when we reached the sands her paws found purchase and we slowly made our way towards the shallows to paddle.

Looking down the length of the beach, I saw that it was decorated with dozens of loving messages etched into the sand. Mostly hearts with names inside, often followed by the year, as if the date was important and would last beyond the next tide. 'Jess and Ellie 2020'. 'The Carlton Family, August 20 xxx'. We read them all as we worked our way north in the direction of Waxholme, where the cliff face is perhaps at its highest.

At night-time, the drop looks impossibly high. You can hear only the raking and spitting of the sea and barely make out the shifting, ill-defined blackness below. When I'd been up there the previous Christmas, deciding, waiting for a decision to click into place, my fall felt as if it would have taken me anywhere. Hard into dirt and rocks, shocked into icy water or with a muffled plop as I descended into molasses. Swallowed up with a slurp and removed from the world. From the beach though, looking up at the cliffs in daylight, they glitter, as if studded with gems. The sea has successfully mined the coastline, wearing it back to the degree that it has exposed an old landfill site, the face now covered with newly exposed refuse. The strata of cans, glass and pieces of unwanted crockery catching the light. Much of it has tumbled down onto the beach to be found by Dean Wilson and posted on his Twitter with the caption 'You're not a pebble, but I like you.'

Looking at the cliffs then, I was reminded of a scratchy old MGM cartoon that I'd often see on TV as a kid, titled *The Little Mole*. It told the story of a short-sighted young mole who would slip out of his hole at every chance he got, to gaze at a beautiful palace in the distance. One day a skunk who worked as a traveling optician strolled past the hole and convinced the little mole to buy some glasses. When he puts them on, he learns that what he'd been looking at all that time hadn't been a palace at all, but a giant rubbish heap. Then he goes for a walk, breaks his glasses and almost drowns, finally washing up on the sands near his home, where his equally blind mother discovers him. The two of them then admire the rubbish heap together, now restored by myopia to its status as a palace, still as there for them as it had always been. Tuned by Anna to see my world as a series of obvious and connected symbols, I explained the plot of this cartoon to Emma.

'Am I the little mole?' I asked her, looking over at the cliff face.

'No,' she said. 'You know that's not a palace.'

'But do you see it the way I see it?'

'I don't think anyone sees this place the way you do.'

We turned away from the cliffs then, heading south and over to the sea, wanting to get our feet in it. To get a sense of the water before we left town and it perhaps wouldn't be available to us again for a while, aware that we could be locked down again at any time. I allowed Millie off her lead and watched as she trotted out into the shallows, where a small wave rushed in and immediately knocked her uncertain legs from under her, sending her over into the water and onto her side. I waded in and picked her up, sandy and dripping, and carried her back to the car. This blessed, loveable wreck.

'It's okay,' I said as we walked, making sure she could see that I was talking to her. 'I've got you.'

Emma opened the rear door and I gently laid Millie on a blanket on the back seat. 'It's okay,' I continued, 'it's okay,'

We got in the car and settled Millie down, then I eased onto the road and travelled along the promenade, heading in the direction of the pier towers. As we got closer, I considered pointing out the spot opposite them where Robert had died.

Perhaps even suggesting that we get out to take a look. But I kept on driving, reminding myself to not be *too much* – too weird too quickly. *I'll save you for next time*, I thought, moving past Robert's resting place and putting my foot down, picking up speed as we headed inland. *I'll save you.*

# Acknowledgments

Before writing these acknowledgments, I was advised to watch as many terrible, overlong and gushing Oscar acceptance speeches as possible, then try not to emulate them. So, let's see how this goes.

A memoir really relies on other people's stories as much as your own, and without the kindness and permission of those people, this book wouldn't exist. In my case, the stories are largely those of my compelling, hilarious and wonderfully complex family. My elder sister Becky, my younger brother Ben, my parents, Janet and Ian, and my late brother Robert, who will remain a part of the family wherever he might be. Their love, openness, and quality of being so writable in the first place have really made this book what it is. It was a joy to get feedback on the manuscript and learn that readers were growing to love my family almost as much as I do. I'd also like to thank the poet Dean Wilson, my brother in Art Rock, Alex Redhead and my beautiful, best and longest standing (but never oldest) friend Zoe MacGechan for allowing me to include them and their words in these pages, as well as for being tremendous humans outside of them.

I need to pay respects to some of the friends, writers and musicians who have been variously and importantly kind, supportive, and provided me with sanctuary when I needed it. There are a lot, so here we go *deep breath* In no particular order, Amina Helal, Fat Roland, Lee Moore, Emma Jane Unsworth, Joe Daly, Wendy and Mike Cook, Thom Hammersley, Paul Fleishman, David Gaffney, Ebba Brooks, Steve Kedie, Benjamin Judge, Rosa Wright, Nick Thompson, Liam Frost, Mark Powell, Jazz Chatfield, Ros Ballinger, Jack Nicholls, Abi Hynes, Simon Buckley, Gaynor Jones and everyone who has ever run Verbose. I must single out Kate Feld and Nija Dalal-Small for taking me under their wings,

# Acknowledgments

including me in The Real Story and changing my life. I bloody love you. Additional thanks to Will Mackie and New Writing North, Arts Council England, Nathan and Laura at Dead Ink Books, everyone at Prestwich Arts Festival and Sara, Aisling and Rosie at Saraband, who made me feel like part of another family. If I've left anyone out, it'll be a result of having cracked my head on a kitchen cupboard door earlier today, and I can only apologise.

Enormous and particular thanks to Jenn Ashworth, my wise, funny and perceptive mentor during the writing of this book and my genuine hero, whose advice is so valuable you could buy a yacht with it. When I had a minor breakdown during the early stages of this manuscript, she fed me an incredible Christmas dinner then took me on a twilight trip to visit a nuclear power station and a failed poet's grave. This was a powerful and sobering restorative. And please, if you're ever lucky enough to meet her, do ask her what her favourite swearword is.

Now, indulge me here, but I'm going to express gratitude for my late, very elderly dog, Millie, who managed to star in and live beyond the completion of this manuscript. While she will never read these words (she was blind, a dog and is, most crucially, dead) I had to honour her, my calamitous, dearly missed, sofa-wrecking companion.

So, now I am crying. Oscar-acceptance crying. So, I'd best wrap this up and finally thank the beautiful, endlessly supportive people who live with me and had to tolerate me writing and ceaselessly talking about this book; my gentle, thoughtful but acerbically funny daughter Effie, and my talented, infinitely understanding partner, Emma Yates-Badley, who knows me better than anyone else alive. You are the loves of my goddamn life.

p.s. God loves Withernsea.

Simor Buckley

**Adam Farrer** is a writer and editor based in Manchester, England, whose work has been published in anthologies and journals. He edits the creative nonfiction journal *The Real Story*, as well as teaching writing workshops and performing at literary events. *Cold Fish Soup* is his first book.

Publisher's note:
*At the time of going to press we have been unable to locate the administrators of the estate of Patrick von Kalckreuth to obtain permission to reproduce the cover painting, despite best efforts. If you have information on this, we would be glad to hear from you.*